STUDY GUIDE

to Accompany

PRINCIPLES OF
MACROECONOMICS

BRIEF SECOND CANADIAN EDITION

N. Gregory Mankiw
HARVARD UNIVERSITY

Ronald D. Kneebone
UNIVERSITY OF CALGARY

Kenneth J. McKenzie
UNIVERSITY OF CALGARY

Nicholas Rowe
CARLETON UNIVERSITY

Peter Fortura
ALGONQUIN COLLEGE

Shahram Manouchehri
GRANT MacEwan COLLEGE

THOMSON
™
NELSON

Australia   Canada   Mexico   Singapore   Spain   United Kingdom   United States

THOMSON
NELSON

Study Guide to Accompany Principles of Macroeconomics,
Brief Second Canadian Edition
by Peter Fortura and Shahram Manouchehri

Editorial Director and Publisher:
Evelyn Veitch

Acquisitions Editor:
Anthony Rezek

Developmental Editor:
Klaus G. Unger

Production Editors:
Emily Ferguson, Bob Kohlmeier

Production Coordinator:
Julie Preston

Compositor:
Computer Composition of Canada

Printer:
Webcom

National Library of Canada Cataloguing in Publication

Fortura, Peter

Study guide to accompany Principles of macroeconomics, brief second Canadian edition / Peter Fortura, Shahram Manouchehri.

Supplement to: Principles of macroeconomics / N. Gregory Mankiw ... [et al.] Brief 2nd Canadian ed.

ISBN 0-17-641555-6

1. Macroeconomics—Problems, exercises, etc. I. Manouchehri, Shahram, 1950– II. Title.

HB172.5.P744 2002a Suppl. 1   339
C2002-905519-9

One must learn by doing the things;
For though you think you know it
You have no certainty, until you try.

Sophocles, c. 496–406 B.C.
Greek playwright
Trachiniae

PREFACE

Economics is a way of thinking. It provides a tool kit for solving problems and making decisions. You may be tempted to learn economics by simply listening to lectures or relying on common sense. Don't be fooled. Economics cannot be learned by osmosis. Learning requires active participation by the student. This means solving problems and answering questions, then looking at the reasons behind both the correct and incorrect answers.

This *Study Guide* was written to accompany the brief edition of the second Canadian edition of *Principles of Macroeconomics*, by N. Gregory Mankiw, Ronald D. Kneebone, Kenneth J. McKenzie, and Nicholas Rowe. It was written with only one audience in mind — you, the student. It is intended to complement the material provided in the text and your instructor's lectures, thereby helping you to be successful in this course.

Objectives of the *Study Guide*

There are three broad objectives to the *Study Guide*. First, it reinforces the text and improves your understanding of the material presented in the text. Second, it provides you with experience in using economic theories and tools to solve actual economic problems — learning by doing! Third, the questions and problems allow you to validate areas of successful learning and to highlight areas needing additional study.

Organization of the *Study Guide*

Each chapter in the *Study Guide* corresponds to a chapter in the brief edition of the second Canadian edition of *Principles of Macroeconomics*. Each *Study Guide* chapter includes the following sections:

I. *Chapter Overview:* This section begins with a description of the purpose of the chapter and of how the chapter fits into the overall framework of the text. The overview also includes helpful hints to guide the student's intuition in understanding the material.

II. *Self-Testing Challenges:* This section begins with true/false questions and multiple-choice questions. These questions provide useful feedback in preparation for an exam, particularly if the student analyzes the right and wrong answers. Next, there are short-answer questions and practice problems, which provide applications and important extensions of the material in the text. The practice problems are generally multiple-step problems, while each short-answer question is generally based on a single topic in the text. The section ends with an advanced critical thinking problem, which applies the economic reasoning and tools developed in the chapter to a real-world problem.

III. *Solutions:* This section provides answers to all of the questions and problems in the *Study Guide*. Explanations are provided for the false responses to the true/false questions.

Use of the *Study Guide*

A study guide is not a substitute for a text. Use this *Study Guide* in conjunction with the *Principles of Macroeconomics* text, not in place of it. How one best uses a study guide is largely a personal matter. Most students will prefer to read through the entire chapter in the text and then work through the *Study Guide*, identifying the areas which need further study and the areas which are already mastered.

Multiple-choice questions tend to be the most commonly used type of exam question. Yet students often encounter difficulties with this type of question because they find that many of the choices differ only slightly. Thus, students should develop and practise strategies for doing multiple-choice questions. The following are some helpful strategies: read each question and all of the choices very carefully — often, only one word is the difference between two of the choices. Eliminate any obviously wrong choices. Mark-up the page with notes, arrows, and diagrams. Remember that the correct answer may not be immediately evident — most questions will require you to analyze numerical and graphical information.

Acknowledgments

I would like to thank Gregory Mankiw for having written such an innovative and lively text, and the Canadian authors for carefully adapting Mankiw's ideas to fit the Canadian experience. Thanks also to David Hakes who wrote the *Principles of Macroeconomics Study Guide* for the U.S. market. His excellent work made producing the Canadian edition a truly enjoyable task. I also thank Klaus Unger, the Developmental Editor, for providing helpful feedback.

Final Thoughts

Economics can be a tremendously exciting and enjoyable field of study. But it can also be intimidating. I hope that this *Study Guide* will improve your understanding of economics, so that you are able to enjoy the subject as much as I do.

Peter Fortura

CONTENTS

Principles of Macroeconomics: Correlation Chart Full and Brief Editions

Chapter 1: Ten Principles of Economics

I. Chapter Overview

A. Context and Purpose

Chapter 1 is the first chapter in a three-chapter section that serves as the introduction to the text. Chapter 1 introduces ten fundamental principles on which the study of economics is based. In a broad sense, the rest of the text is an elaboration on these ten principles. Chapter 2 will develop how economists approach problems, while Chapter 3 will explain how individuals and countries gain from trade.

The purpose of Chapter 1 is to lay out ten economic principles that will serve as building blocks for the rest of the text. The ten principles can be grouped into three categories: how people make decisions, how people interact, and how the economy works as a whole. Throughout the text, references will repeatedly be made to these ten principles.

B. Helpful Hints

1. *Place yourself in the story.* Throughout the text, most economic situations will be composed of economic actors — buyers and sellers, borrowers and lenders, firms and workers, and so on. When you are asked to address how any economic actor would respond to economic incentives, place yourself in the story as the buyer or the seller, the borrower or the lender, the producer or the consumer. Don't think of yourself always as the buyer (a natural tendency) or always as the seller. You will find that your role playing will usually produce the right response once you learn to think like an economist — which is the topic of the next chapter.

2. *Trade is not a zero-sum game.* Some people see an exchange in terms of winners and losers. Their reaction to trade is that, after the sale, if the seller is happy, the buyer must be sad because the seller must have taken something from the buyer. That is, they view trade as a *zero-sum game* where what one gains the other must have lost. They fail to see that both parties to a voluntary transaction gain because each party is allowed to specialize in what it can produce most efficiently, and then trade for items that are produced more efficiently by others. Nobody loses, because trade is voluntary. Therefore, a government policy that limits trade reduces the potential gains from trade.

3. *An externality can be positive.* Because the classic example of an externality is pollution, it is easy to think of an externality as a cost that lands on a bystander. However, an externality can be positive in that it can be a benefit that lands on a bystander. For example, education is often cited as a product that emits a positive externality because when your neighbour educates herself, she is likely to be more reasonable, responsible, productive, and politically astute. In short, she is a better neighbour. Positive externalities, just as much as negative externalities, may be a reason for the government to intervene to promote efficiency.

II. Self-Testing Challenges

A. True/False Questions

_____1.   When the government redistributes income with taxes and welfare, the economy becomes more efficient.

_____2.   When economists say, "There is no such thing as a free lunch," they mean that all economic decisions involve tradeoffs.

_____3.   Adam Smith's "invisible hand" concept describes how corporate business reaches into the pockets of consumers like an "invisible hand."

_____4.   Rational people act only when the marginal benefit of the action exceeds the marginal cost.

_____5.   Canada will benefit economically if we eliminate trade with Asian countries because we will be forced to produce more of our own cars and clothes.

_____6.   When a jet flies overhead, the noise it generates is an externality.

_____7.   A tax on beer raises the price of beer and provides an incentive for consumers to drink more.

_____8.   An unintended consequence of government support for higher education is that low tuition provides an incentive for some people to attend universities even if they have little desire to learn anything.

_____9.   Sue is better at cleaning and Bob is better at cooking. It will take fewer hours to eat and clean if Bob specializes in cooking and Sue specializes in cleaning than if they share the household duties evenly.

_____10. High and persistent inflation is caused by excessive growth in the quantity of money in the economy.

_____11. In the short run, a reduction in inflation tends to cause a reduction in unemployment.

_____12. An auto manufacturer should continue to produce additional automobiles as long as the firm is profitable, even if the cost of the additional units exceed the price received.

_____13. An individual farmer is likely to have _market power_ in the market for wheat.

_____14. To a student, the opportunity cost of going to a basketball game would include the price of the ticket and the value of the time that could have been spent studying.

_____15. Workers in Canada have a relatively high standard of living because Canada has a relatively high minimum wage.

B. Multiple-Choice Questions

1. Which of the following involve(s) a tradeoff?
   a. buying a new car
   b. going to university
   c. watching a football game on Saturday afternoon
   d. taking a nap
   e. all of the above involve tradeoffs

2. Tradeoffs are required because wants are unlimited and resources are
   a. efficient.
   b. economical.
   c. scarce.
   d. unlimited.
   e. marginal.

3. Economics is the study of
   a. how to fully satisfy our unlimited wants.
   b. how society manages its scarce resources.
   c. how to reduce our wants until we are satisfied.
   d. how to avoid having to make tradeoffs.
   e. how society manages its unlimited resources.

4. A rational person does not act unless
   a. the action makes money for the person.
   b. the action is ethical.
   c. the action produces marginal costs that exceed marginal benefits.
   d. the action produces marginal benefits that exceed marginal costs.
   e. none of the above.

5. Raising taxes and increasing welfare payments
   a. proves that there is such a thing as a free lunch.
   b. reduces market power.
   c. improves efficiency at the expense of equity.
   d. improves equity at the expense of efficiency.
   e. none of the above.

6. Suppose you find $20. If you choose to use the $20 to go to a hockey game, your opportunity cost of going to the game is
   a. nothing, because you found the money.
   b. $20 (because you could have used the $20 to buy other things).
   c. $20 (because you could have used the $20 to buy other things) plus the value of the time spent at the game.
   d. $20 (because you could have used the $20 to buy other things) plus the value of the time spent at the game, plus the cost of the soft drink and hot dog you consumed at the game.
   e. none of the above.

7. Foreign trade
   a. allows a country to have a greater variety of products at a lower cost than if it tried to produce everything at home.
   b. allows a country to avoid tradeoffs.
   c. makes a country more equitable.
   d. increases the scarcity of resources.
   e. none of the above.

8. Since people respond to incentives, we would expect that, if the average salary of accountants increases by 50% while the average salary of teachers increases by 20%,
   a. students will shift majors from education to accounting.
   b. students will shift majors from accounting to education.
   c. fewer students will attend university.
   d. none of the above.

9. Which of the following activities is most likely to produce an externality?
   a. A student sits at home and watches TV.
   b. A student has a party in her student residence room.
   c. A student reads a novel for pleasure.
   d. A student eats a hamburger in the student union cafeteria.

10. Which of the following products would be *least* capable of producing an externality?
    a. cigarettes
    b. stereo equipment
    c. inoculations against disease
    d. education
    e. food

11. Which of the following situations describes the greatest *market power*?
    a. a farmer's impact on the price of corn
    b. Saab's impact on the price of autos
    c. Microsoft's impact on the price of desktop operating systems
    d. a student's impact on university tuition

12. Which of the following statements is true about a market economy?
    a. Market participants act as if guided by an "invisible hand" to produce outcomes that maximize social welfare.
    b. Taxes help prices communicate costs and benefits to producers and consumers.
    c. With a large enough computer, central planners could guide production more efficiently than markets.
    d. The strength of a market system is that it tends to distribute resources evenly across consumers.

13. According to Adam Smith's "invisible hand,"
    a. government plays a behind-the-scenes role in making a market economy work efficiently.
    b. individuals who are concerned about the public good will almost invisibly promote increased social welfare.
    c. free markets require only a little intervention to operate smoothly.
    d. many buyers and sellers acting independently out of self-interest can promote general economic well-being without even realizing it.
    e. all of the above.

14. Workers in Canada enjoy a high standard of living because
    a. unions in Canada keep the wage high.
    b. we have protected our industry from foreign competition.
    c. Canada has a high minimum wage.
    d. workers in Canada are highly productive.
    e. none of the above.

15. High and persistent inflation is caused by
    a. unions increasing wages too much.
    b. OPEC raising the price of oil too much.
    c. governments increasing the quantity of money too much.
    d. regulations raising the cost of production too much.

16. The Phillips curve suggests that
    a. an increase in inflation temporarily increases unemployment.
    b. a decrease in inflation temporarily increases unemployment.
    c. inflation and unemployment are unrelated in the short run.
    d. none of the above.

17. An increase in the price of beef provides information that
    a. tells consumers to buy more beef.
    b. tells consumers to buy less pork.
    c. tells producers to produce more beef.
    d. provides no information because prices in a market system are managed by planning boards.

18. You have spent $1000 building a hot dog stand based on estimates of sales of $2000. The hot dog stand is nearly completed but now you estimate total sales to be only $800. You can complete the hot dog stand for another $300. Should you complete the hot dog stand?
    a. Yes.
    b. No.
    c. There is not enough information to answer this question.

19. Referring to question 18, your decision rule should be to complete the hot dog stand as long as the cost to complete the stand is less than
    a. $100.
    b. $300.
    c. $500.
    d. $800.
    e. none of the above.

20. Which of the following is not part of the opportunity cost of going on vacation?
    a. the money you could have made if you had stayed home and worked
    b. the money you spent on food
    c. the money you spent on airplane tickets
    d. the money you spent on a Broadway show

21. Productivity can be increased by
    a. raising minimum wage.
    b. raising union wages.
    c. improving the education of workers.
    d. restricting trade with foreign countries.

C. Short-Answer Questions

1. Is air scarce? Is clean air scarce? _____
    _____
    _____

2. What is the opportunity cost of saving some of your paycheque? _____
    _____
    _____

3. Why is there a tradeoff between equity and efficiency? _____
    _____
    _____

4. Water is necessary for life. Diamonds are not. Is the marginal benefit of an additional glass of water greater or less than an additional one-carat diamond? Why? _____
    _____
    _____

5. Your car needs to be repaired. You have already paid $500 to have the transmission fixed, but it still doesn't work properly. You can sell your car "as is" for $2000. If your car were fixed, you could sell it for $2500. Your car can be fixed with a guarantee for another $300. Should you repair your car? Why? _____
    _____
    _____

6. Why do you think air bags have reduced deaths from auto crashes less than we had hoped? _____

_____

_____

7. Suppose one country is better at producing agricultural products (because they have more fertile land) while another country is better at producing manufactured goods (they have a better educational system and more engineers). If each country produced their specialty and traded, would there be more or less total output than if each country produced all of their agricultural and manufacturing needs? Why? _____

_____

_____

8. In *The Wealth of Nations* Adam Smith said, "It is not by the benevolence of the baker that you receive your bread." What do you think he meant? _____

_____

_____

9. If we save more and use it to build more physical capital, productivity will rise and we will have rising standards of living in the future. What is the opportunity cost of future growth? _____

_____

_____

10. If the government printed twice as much money, what do you think would happen to prices and output if the economy were already producing at maximum capacity? _____

_____

_____

11. A goal for a society is to distribute resources equitably or fairly. How would you distribute resources if everyone were equally talented and worked equally hard? What if people had different talents and some people worked hard while others didn't? _____

_____

12. Who is more self-interested, the buyer or the seller? _____

_____

_____

13. Why might government deficits slow a country's growth rate? _____

_____

_____

D. Practice Problems

1. People respond to incentives. Governments can alter incentives and, hence, behaviour with public policy. However, sometimes public policy generates unintended consequences by producing results that were not anticipated. Try to find an unintended consequence of each of the following public policies.

    a. To help the "working poor," the government raises the minimum wage to $25 per hour. _____

    _____

    _____

    b. To help the homeless, the government places rent controls on apartments restricting rent to $10 per month. _____

    _____

    _____

    c. To limit the consumption of gasoline, the government raises the tax on gasoline by $2.00 per litre. _____

    _____

    _____

    d. To reduce the consumption of drugs, the government makes drugs illegal. _____

    _____

    _____

    _____

    e. To raise the population of wolves, the government prohibits the killing of wolves. _____

    _____

2. Opportunity cost is what you give up to get an item. Since there is no such thing as a free lunch, what would likely be given up to obtain each of the items listed below?

    a. Susan can work full time or go to university. She chooses university. _____

    _____

    _____

    b. Susan can work full time or go to university. She chooses work. _____

    _____

    _____

    _____

    _____

c. Farmer Jones has 100 hectares of land. He can plant corn, which yields 100 tonnes per hectare, or he can plant beans, which yield 40 tonnes per hectare. He chooses to plant corn. _____

d. Farmer Jones has 100 hectares of land. He can plant corn, which yields 100 tonnes per hectare, or he can plant beans, which yield 40 tonnes per hectare. He chooses to plant beans. _____

e. In (a) and (b) above, and (c) and (d) above, which is the opportunity cost of which — university for work or work for university? Corn for beans or beans for corn? _____
_____
_____

E. Advanced Critical Thinking

Suppose your university decides to lower the cost of parking on campus by reducing the price of a parking sticker from $200 per semester to $5 per semester.

1. What do you think would happen to the number of students desiring to park their cars on campus? _____
_____
_____

2. What do you think would happen to the amount of time it would take to find a parking place? _____
_____
_____

3. Thinking in terms of opportunity cost, would the lower price of a parking sticker necessarily lower the true cost of parking? _____
_____
_____

4. Would the opportunity cost of parking be the same for students with no outside employment and students with jobs earning $15 per hour? _____
_____
_____

III. Solutions

A. True/False Questions

1. F; the economy becomes less efficient because it decreases the incentive to work hard.
2. T
3. F; the "invisible hand" refers to how markets guide self-interested people to create desirable social outcomes.

4. T
5. F; all countries gain from voluntary trade.
6. T
7. F; higher prices reduce the quantity demanded.
8. T
9. T
10. T
11. F; a reduction in inflation tends to raise unemployment.
12. F; a manufacturer should produce as long as the marginal benefit exceeds the marginal cost.
13. F; a single farmer is too small to influence the market.
14. T
15. F; workers in Canada have a high standard of living because they are productive.

B. Multiple-Choice Questions

1.	e	7.	a	12.	a	17.	c
2.	c	8.	a	13.	d	18.	a
3.	b	9.	b	14.	d	19.	d
4.	d	10.	e	15.	c	20.	b
5.	d	11.	c	16.	b	21.	c
6.	c						

C. Short-Answer Questions

1. No, you don't have to give up anything to get it. Yes, you can't have as much as you want without giving up something to get it (pollution equipment on cars, etc.).

2. The items you could have enjoyed had you spent it (current consumption).

3. Taxes and welfare make us more equal but reduce incentives for hard work, lowering total output.

4. The marginal benefit of another glass of water is generally lower because we have so much water that one more glass is of little value. The opposite is true for diamonds.

5. Yes, because the marginal benefit of fixing the car is $2500 – $2000 = $500 and the marginal cost is $300. The original repair payment is not relevant.

6. The cost of an accident was lowered. This changed incentives so people drive faster and have more accidents.

7. There would be more total output if they specialize and trade because each is doing what it does most efficiently.

8. The baker produces the best bread possible, not out of kindness, but because it is in his best interest to do so. Self-interest can maximize social welfare.

9. We must give up consumption today.

10. Spending would double but since the quantity of output would remain the same, prices would double.

11. Fairness would require that everyone get an equal share. Fairness would require that people not get an equal share.

12. They are equally self-interested. The seller will sell to the highest bidder and the buyer will buy from the lowest offer.

13. Deficits absorb saving which reduces society's investment in capital.

D. Practice Problems

1. a. Many would want to work at $25/hour but few firms would want to hire low productivity workers at this wage; therefore, it would simply create unemployment.

   b. Many renters would want to rent an apartment at $10/month, but few landlords could produce an apartment at this price, therefore, this rent control would create more homelessness.

   c. Higher gas prices would reduce the kilometres driven. This would lower auto accidents, put less wear and tear on roads and cars, and reduce the demand for cars and road repairs.

   d. This raises the price of drugs and makes selling them more profitable. This creates more drug sellers and increases violence as they fight to protect their turf.

   e. Restrictions on killing wolves reduce the population of animals upon which wolves may feed — rabbits, deer, etc.

2. a. She gives up income from work (and must pay tuition).

   b. She gives up a university degree and the increase in income throughout life that it would have brought her (but doesn't have to pay tuition).

   c. He gives up 4000 tonnes of beans.

   d. He gives up 10 000 tonnes of corn.

e. Each is the opportunity cost of the other because each decision requires giving something up.

E. Advanced Critical Thinking

1. More students would wish to park on campus.

2. It would take much longer to find a parking place.

3. No, because we would have to factor in the value of our time spent looking for a parking place.

4. No. Students who could be earning money working are giving up more while looking for a parking place than those with no outside employment. Therefore, their opportunity cost is higher.

Chapter 2: Thinking Like an Economist

I. Chapter Overview

A. Context and Purpose

Chapter 2 is the second chapter in a three-chapter section that serves as the introduction of the text. Chapter 1 introduced ten principles of economics that will be revisited throughout the text. Chapter 2 develops how economists approach problems, while Chapter 3 will explain how individuals and countries gain from trade.

The purpose of Chapter 2 is to familiarize you with how economists approach economic problems. With practice, you will learn how to approach similar problems in this dispassionate systematic way. You will see how economists employ the scientific method, the role of assumptions in model building, and the application of two specific economic models. You will also learn the important distinction between two roles economists can play: as scientists when we try to explain the economic world and as policymakers when we try to improve it.

B. Helpful Hints

1. *Opportunity costs are not usually constant along a production possibilities frontier.* Notice that the production possibilities frontier shown in the following graph is bowed outward. It shows the production tradeoffs for an economy that produces only paper and pencils.

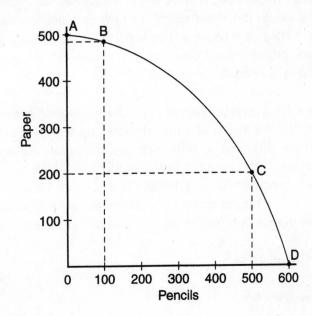

If we start at the point where the economy is using all of its resources to produce paper, producing 100 units of pencils only requires a tradeoff or an opportunity cost of 25 units of paper (point A to point B). This is because when we move resources from paper to pencil production, we first move those resources best suited for pencil production and poorly suited for paper production. Therefore, pencil production increases with very little decrease in paper production. However, if the economy were operating at point C, the opportunity cost of an additional 100 pencils (point C to D) is 200 units of paper. This is because we now move resources toward pencil production that were extremely well suited for paper production and are poorly suited for pencil production. Therefore, as we produce more and more of any particular good, the opportunity cost per unit tends to rise because resources are specialized. That is, resources are not equally well suited for producing each output.

The argument above applies when moving either direction on the production possibilities frontier. For example, if we start at point D (maximum production of pencils) a small reduction in pencil production (100 units) releases enough resources to increase production of paper by a large amount (200 units). However, moving from point B to point A only increases paper production by 25 units.

2. *A production possibilities frontier only shows the choices available — not which point of production is best.* A common mistake made by students when using production possibilities frontiers is to look at a production possibilities frontier and suggest that a point somewhere near the middle "looks best." Students make this subjective judgement because the middle point appears to provide the biggest total number of units of production of the two goods. However, ask yourself the following question: Using the production possibilities frontier in the previous graph, what production point would be best if paper were worth $10 per sheet and pencils were worth 1 cent per dozen? We would move our resources toward paper production. What if paper were worth 1 cent per sheet and pencils were worth $50 each? We would move our resources toward pencil production. Clearly, what we actually choose to produce depends on the price of each good. Therefore, a production possibilities frontier only provides the choices available; it alone cannot determine which choice is best.

3. *Economic disagreement is interesting but economic consensus is more important.* Economists have a reputation for disagreeing with one another because we tend to highlight our differences. While our disagreements are interesting to us, the matters on which we agree are more important to you. There are a great number of economic principles for which there is near unanimous support from the economics profession. The aim of this text is to concentrate on the areas of agreement within the profession as opposed to the areas of disagreement.

II. Self-Testing Challenges

A. True/False Questions

_____1.   Economic models must mirror reality or they are of no value.

_____2.   Assumptions make the world easier to understand because they simplify reality and focus our attention.

_____3.   It is reasonable to assume that the world is composed of only one person when modeling international trade.

_____4.   When people act as scientists, they must try to be objective.

_____5.   If an economy is operating on its production possibilities frontier, it must be using its resources efficiently.

_____6.   If an economy is operating on its production possibilities frontier, it must produce less of one good if it produces more of another.

_____7.   Points outside the production possibilities frontier are attainable but inefficient.

_____8.   If an economy were experiencing substantial unemployment, the economy is producing inside the production possibilities frontier.

_____9.   The production possibilities frontier is bowed outward because the tradeoffs between the production of any two goods are constant.

_____10.   An advance in production technology would cause the production possibilities curve to shift outward.

_____11.   Macroeconomics is concerned with the study of how households and firms make decisions and how they interact in specific markets.

_____12.   The statement, "An increase in inflation tends to cause unemployment to fall in the short run," is normative.

_____13.   When economists make positive statements, they are more likely to be acting as scientists.

_____14.   Normative statements can be refuted with evidence.

_____15.   Economists may appear to disagree more than they actually do because they have different hunches about the validity of alternative theories.

B. Multiple-Choice Questions

1.   The scientific method requires that
   a.   the scientist use test tubes and have a clean lab.
   b.   the scientist be objective.
   c.   the scientist use precision equipment.
   d.   only incorrect theories are tested.
   e.   only correct theories are tested.

2.   Which of the following is most likely to produce scientific evidence about a theory?
   a.   An economist employed by the Canadian Auto Workers union doing research on the impact of trade restrictions.
   b.   A radio talk show host collecting data on how capital markets respond to taxation.

    c. A tenured economist employed at a leading university analyzing the impact of bank regulations on rural lending.

    d. A lawyer employed by General Motors addressing the impact of air bags on passenger safety.

3. Which of the following statements regarding the circular-flow diagram is true?
    a. The factors of production are owned by households.
    b. If Susan works for Bell Canada and receives a paycheque, the transaction takes place in the market for goods and services.
    c. If Corel Corporation sells a computer software package, the transaction takes place in the market for factors of production.
    d. The factors of production are owned by firms.
    e. None of the above.

4. In which of the following cases is the assumption most reasonable?
    a. To estimate the speed at which a beachball falls, a physicist assumes that it falls in a vacuum.
    b. To address the impact of money growth on inflation, an economist assumes that money is strictly coins.
    c. To address the impact of taxes on income distribution, an economist assumes that everyone earns the same income.
    d. To address the benefits of trade, an economist assumes that there are two people and two goods.

5. Economic models are
    a. created to duplicate reality.
    b. built with assumptions.
    c. usually made of wood and plastic.
    d. useless if they are simple.

6. Which of the following is not a factor of production?
    a. land
    b. labour
    c. capital
    d. money
    e. all of the above

7. Points on the production possibilities frontier are
    a. efficient.
    b. inefficient.
    c. unattainable.
    d. normative.
    e. none of the above.

8. Which of the following will not shift a country's production possibilities frontier outward?
   a. an increase in the capital stock
   b. an advance in technology
   c. a reduction in unemployment
   d. an increase in the labour force

9. Economic growth is depicted by
   a. a movement along a production possibilities frontier toward capital goods.
   b. a shift in the production possibilities frontier outward.
   c. a shift in the production possibilities frontier inward.
   d. a movement from inside the curve toward the curve.

Use the following graph to answer questions 10-13.

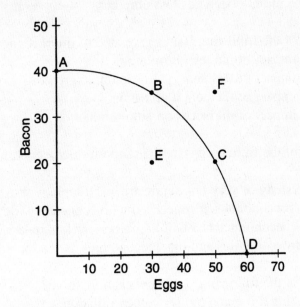

10. If the economy is operating at point C, the opportunity cost of producing an additional 15 units of bacon is
    a. 10 units of eggs.
    b. 20 units of eggs.
    c. 30 units of eggs.
    d. 40 units of eggs.
    e. 50 units of eggs.

11. If the economy is operating at point E
    a. the opportunity cost of 20 additional units of eggs is 10 units of bacon.
    b. the opportunity cost of 20 additional units of eggs is 20 units of bacon.
    c. the opportunity cost of 20 additional units of eggs is 30 units of bacon.
    d. 20 additional units of eggs can be produced with no impact on bacon production.

12. Point F represents
    a. a combination of production that can be reached if we reduce the production of eggs by 20 units.
    b. a combination of production that is inefficient because there are unemployed resources.
    c. a combination of production that can be reached if there is a sufficient advance in technology.
    d. none of the above.

13. As we move from point A to point D
    a. the opportunity cost of eggs in terms of bacon is constant.
    b. the opportunity cost of eggs in terms of bacon falls.
    c. the opportunity cost of eggs in terms of bacon rises.
    d. the economy becomes more efficient.
    e. the economy becomes less efficient.

14. Which of the following issues is related to microeconomics?
    a. the impact of money on inflation
    b. the impact of technology on economic growth
    c. the impact of the deficit on saving
    d. the impact of oil prices on auto production

15. Which of the following statements about microeconomics and macroeconomics is not true?
    a. The study of very large industries is a topic within macroeconomics.
    b. Macroeconomics is concerned with economy-wide phenomena.
    c. Microeconomics is a building block for macroeconomics.
    d. Microeconomics and macroeconomics cannot be entirely separated.

16. Which of the following statements is normative?
    a. Printing too much money causes inflation.
    b. People work harder if the wage is higher.
    c. The unemployment rate should be lower.
    d. Large government deficits cause an economy to grow more slowly.

17. In making which of the following statements is an economist acting more like a scientist?
    a. A reduction in unemployment benefits will reduce the unemployment rate.
    b. The unemployment rate should be reduced because unemployment robs individuals of their dignity.
    c. The rate of inflation should be reduced because it robs the elderly of their savings.
    d. The government should increase subsidies to universities because the future of our country depends on education.

18. Positive statements are
    a. microeconomic.
    b. macroeconomic.
    c. statements of prescription that involve value judgements.
    d. statements of description that can be tested.

19. Suppose two economists are arguing about policies that deal with unemployment. One economist says, "The government should fight unemployment because it is the greatest social evil." The other economists responds, "Hogwash. Inflation is the greatest social evil." These economists
    a. disagree because they have different scientific judgements.
    b. disagree because they have different values.
    c. disagree because at least one of them is a charlatan or a crank.
    d. really don't disagree at all. It just looks that way.

20. Suppose two economists are arguing about policies that deal with unemployment. One economist says, "The government could lower unemployment by one percentage point if it would just increase government spending by 5 billion dollars." The other economist responds, "Hogwash. If the government spent an additional 5 billion dollars, it would reduce unemployment by only one-tenth of one percent, and that effect would only be temporary!" These economists
    a. disagree because they have different scientific judgements.
    b. disagree because they have different values.
    c. disagree because at least one of them is a charlatan or a crank.
    d. really don't disagree at all. It just looks that way.

C. Short-Answer Questions

1. Describe the scientific method. _____
   _____

2. What is the role of assumptions in any science? _____
   _____

3. Is a more realistic model always better? _____
   _____
   _____

4. Why does a production possibilities frontier have a negative slope (slope down and to the right)? _____
   _____
   _____

5. Why is the production possibilities frontier bowed outward? _____
   _____
   _____

6. What are the two subfields within economics? Which is more likely to be a building block of the other? Why? _____

_____

_____

_____

7. When an economist makes a normative statement, are they more likely to be acting as a scientist or a policymaker? Why? _____

_____

_____

_____

8. Which statements are testable: positive statements or normative statements? Why? _____

_____

9. Name two reasons why economists disagree. _____

_____

_____

10. Name two economic propositions on which more than 90% of economists agree. ____

_____

_____

D. Practice Problems

1. Identify the parts of the circular-flow diagram immediately involved in the following transactions.

    a. Mary buys a car from General Motors for $25 000. _____

    _____

    _____

    _____

    _____

    b. General Motors pays Joe $5000/month for work on the assembly line. _____

    _____

    _____

    _____

    c. Joe gets a $15 hair cut. _____

    _____

    _____

    _____

d. Mary receives $10 000 of dividends on her General Motors stock. _____

_____

_____

_____

_____

2. The following table provides information about the production possibilities frontier of Athletic Country.

Bats	Rackets
0	420
100	400
200	360
300	300
400	200
500	0

a. Plot and connect these points to create Athletic Country's production possibilities frontier.

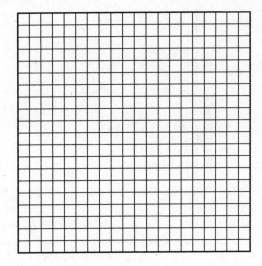

b. If Athletic Country currently produces 100 bats and 400 rackets, what is the opportunity cost of an additional 100 bats? _____

_____

c. If Athletic Country currently produces 300 bats and 300 rackets, what is the opportunity cost of an additional 100 bats? _____

_____

d. Why does the additional production of 100 bats in part (c) cause a greater tradeoff than the additional production of 100 bats in part (b)?_____
_____
_____
_____

e. Suppose Athletic Country is currently producing 200 bats and 200 rackets. How many additional bats could they produce without giving up any rackets? How many additional rackets could they produce without giving up any bats?_____
_____
_____

f. Is the production of 200 bats and 200 rackets efficient? Explain._____
_____
_____

3. The following production possibilities frontier shows the available tradeoffs between consumption goods and capital goods. Suppose two countries face the identical production possibilities frontier shown below.

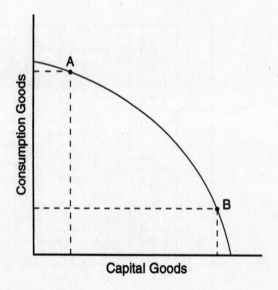

a. Suppose Party Country chooses to produce at point A while Parsimonious Country chooses to produce at point B. Which country will experience more growth in the future? Why?_____
_____
_____

b. In this model, what is the opportunity cost of future growth?_____
_____

c. Demonstrate the impact of growth on a production possibilities frontier such as the one shown above. Would the production possibilities frontier for Parsimonious Country shift more or less than that for Party Country? Why?_____

_____

d. Show the shift in the production possibilities curve if there was an increase in technology that only affected the production of capital goods.

e. Does the shift in part (d) above imply that all additional production must be in the form of capital goods? Why?_____

_____

E. Advanced Critical Thinking

You are watching the National news program on CBC. There is a discussion of the pros and cons of free trade (lack of obstructions to international trade). For balance, there are two economists present — one in support of free trade and one opposed. Your roommate says, "Those economists have no idea what's going on. They can't agree on anything. One says free trade makes us rich. The other says it will drive us into poverty. If the experts don't know, how is the average person ever going to know whether free trade is best?"

1. Can you give your roommate any insight into why economists might disagree on this issue?_____

_____

_____

_____

2. Suppose you discover that 93% of economists believe that free trade is generally best (which is the greatest agreement on any single issue). Could you now give a more precise answer as to why economists might disagree on this issue?_____

_____

_____

_____

3. What if you later discovered that the economist opposed to free trade worked for a labour union. Would that help you explain why there appears to be a difference of opinion on this issue?_____

_____

_____

_____

III. Solutions

A. True/False Questions

1. F; economic models are simplifications of reality.
2. T
3. F; there must be at least two individuals for trade.
4. T
5. T
6. T
7. F; points outside the production possibilities frontier cannot yet be attained.
8. T
9. F; it is bowed outward because the tradeoffs are not constant.
10. T
11. F; macroeconomics is the study of economy-wide phenomena.
12. F; this statement is positive.

13. T
14. F; normative statements cannot be refuted.
15. T

B. Multiple-Choice Questions

1. b	6. d	11. d	16. c
2. c	7. a	12. c	17. a
3. a	8. c	13. c	18. d
4. d	9. b	14. d	19. b
5. b	10. b	15. a	20. a

C. Short-Answer Questions

1. The dispassionate development and testing of theory by observing, testing, and observing again.

2. To simplify reality so that we can focus our thinking on what is actually important.

3. Not necessarily. Realistic models are more complex. They may be confusing and they may fail to focus on what is important.

4. Because if an economy is operating efficiently, production choices have opportunity costs. If we want more of one thing, we must have less of another.

5. Because resources are specialized and thus are not equally well suited for producing different outputs.

6. Microeconomics and macroeconomics. Microeconomics is more of a building block of macro because when we address macro issues (say unemployment) we have to consider how individuals respond to work incentives such as wages and welfare.

7. As a policymaker because normative statements are prescriptions about what ought to be and are somewhat based on value judgements.

8. Positive statements are statements of fact and are refutable by examining evidence.

9. Economists may have different scientific judgements. Economists may have different values.

10. A ceiling on rents reduces the quantity and quality of housing available. Tariffs and import quotas usually reduce general economic welfare.

D. Practice Problems

1. a. $25 000 of spending from households to market for goods and services. Car moves from market for goods and services to households. $25 000 of revenue from market for goods and services to firms while car moves from firms to market for goods and services.

    b. $5000 of wages from firms to market for factors of production. Inputs move from market for factors of production to firms. Labour moves from households to market for factors of production while $5000 income moves from market for factors to households.

    c. $15 of spending from households to market for goods and services. Service moves from market for goods and services to households. Service moves from firms to market for goods and services in return for $15 revenue.

    d. $10 000 of profit from firms to market for factors of production. Inputs move from market for factors of production to firms. Capital services move from households to market for factors of production in return for $10 000 income.

2. a.

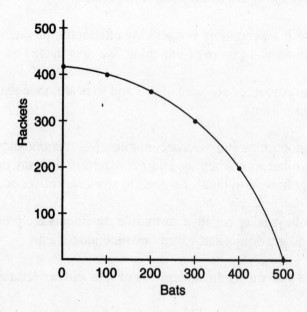

    b. 40 rackets.

    c. 100 rackets.

    d. Because as we produce more bats, the resources best suited for making bats are already being used. Therefore, it takes even more resources to produce 100 bats and greater reductions in racket production.

e. 200 bats. 160 rackets.

f. No. Resources were not used efficiently if production can be increased with no opportunity cost.

3. a. Parsimonious Country. Capital (plant and equipment) is a factor of production and producing more of it now will increase future production.

b. Fewer consumption goods are produced now.

c.

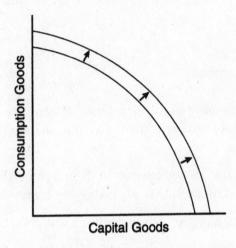

The production possibilities curve will shift more for Parsimonious Country because they have experienced a greater increase in factors of production (capital).

d.

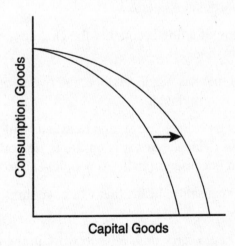

e. No, the outward shift improves choices available for both consumption and capital goods.

E. Advanced Critical Thinking

1. Economists may have different scientific judgements. Economists may have different values.

2. Those opposed to free trade are likely to have different values. There is not much disagreement on this issue within the mainstream economics profession.

3. Yes. It suggests that impediments to international trade may benefit some groups (unionized labour) but these impediments are unlikely to benefit the public in general. Supporters of these policies are promoting their own interests.

IV. Appendix

A. True/False Questions

_____1.   When graphing in the coordinate system, the x-coordinate tells us the horizontal location while the y-coordinate tells us the vertical location of the point.

_____2.   When a line slopes upward in the x-, y-coordinate system, the two variables measured on each axis are positively correlated.

_____3.   Price and quantity demanded for most goods are positively related.

_____4.   If three variables are related, one of them must be held constant when graphing the other two in the x-, y-coordinate system.

_____5.   If three variables are related, a change in the variable not represented on the x-, y-coordinate system will cause a movement along the curve drawn in the x-, y-coordinate system.

_____6.   The slope of a line is equal to the change in y divided by the change in x along the line.

_____7.   When a line has negative slope, the two variables measured on each axis are positively correlated.

_____8.   There is a positive correlation between lying down and death. If we conclude from this evidence that it is unsafe to lie down, we have an omitted variable problem because critically ill people tend to lie down.

_____9.   Reverse causality means that while we think A causes B, B may actually cause A.

_____10. Since people carry umbrellas to work in the morning and it rains later in the afternoon, carrying umbrellas must cause rain.

B. Practice Problems

1. The following ordered pairs of price and quantity demanded describe Joe's demand for cups of gourmet coffee:

Price per cup of coffee	Quantity demanded of coffee
$5	2 cups
$4	4 cups
$3	6 cups
$2	8 cups
$1	10 cups

a. Plot and connect the ordered pairs on the graph provided below.

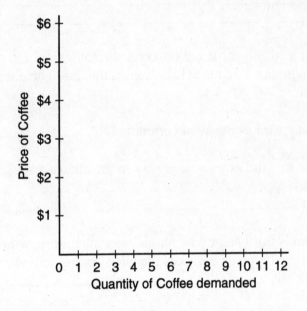

b. What is the slope of Joe's demand curve for coffee in the price range of $5 and $4? _____

c. What is the slope of Joe's demand curve for coffee in the price range of $2 and $1? _____

d. Are the price of coffee and Joe's quantity demanded of coffee positively correlated or negatively correlated? How can you tell? _____
_____
_____

e. If the price of coffee moves from $2 per cup to $4 per cup, what happens to the quantity demanded? Is this a movement along a curve or a shift in the curve?
_____
_____

f. Suppose Joe's income doubles from \$20 000 per year to \$40 000 per year. Now the following ordered pairs describe Joe's demand for gourmet coffee. Plot these ordered pairs on the graph provided in part (a) above.

Price per cup of coffee	Quantity demanded of coffee
\$5	4 cups
\$4	6 cups
\$3	8 cups
\$2	10 cups
\$1	12 cups

g. Did the doubling of Joe's income cause a movement along his demand curve or a shift in his demand curve? Why?_____

_____

_____

2. An alien lands on earth and observes the following: On mornings when people carry umbrellas, it tends to rain later in the day. The alien concludes that umbrellas cause rain.

a. What error has the alien committed?_____

b. What role did *expectations* play in the alien's error?

_____

_____

c. If rain is truly caused by humidity, temperature, wind currents and so on, what additional type of error has the alien committed when it decided that umbrellas cause rain?_____

V. Solutions for Appendix

A. True/False Questions

1. T
2. T
3. F; they are negatively correlated.
4. T
5. F; a change in a variable not represented on the graph will cause a shift in the curve.
6. T
7. F; negative slope implies negative correlation.
8. T
9. T
10. F; this is an example of reverse causation.

B. Practice Problems

1. a.

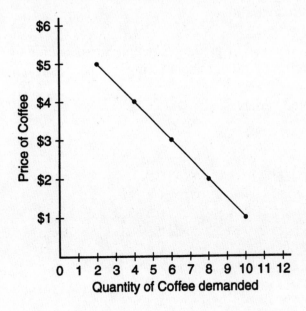

b. –1/2

c. –1/2

d. Negatively correlated. Because an increase in price is associated with a decrease in quantity demanded. That is, the demand curve slopes negatively.

e. Decrease by 4 cups. Movement along curve.

f.

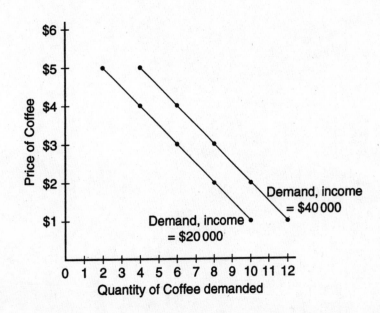

g. Shift in curve because a variable changed (income) that is not measured on either axis.

2. a. Reverse causality.

   b. Since rain can be predicted, people's expectation of rain causes them to carry umbrellas before it rains, making it appear as if umbrellas cause rain.

   c. Omitted variables.

Chapter 3: Interdependence and the Gains from Trade

I. Chapter Overview

A. Context and Purpose

Chapter 3 is the third chapter in the three-chapter section that serves as the introduction of the text. The first chapter introduced ten fundamental principles of economics. The second chapter developed how economists approach problems. This chapter shows how people and countries gain from trade (which is one of the ten principles discussed in Chapter 1).

The purpose of Chapter 3 is to demonstrate how everyone can gain from trade. Trade allows people to specialize in the production of things for which they have a comparative advantage and then trade for things other people produce. Because of specialization, total output rises and through trade we are all able to share in the bounty. This is as true for countries as it is for individuals. Since everyone can gain from trade, restrictions on trade tend to reduce welfare.

B. Helpful Hints

1. *A step-by-step example of comparative advantage.* What follows is an example that will demonstrate most of the concepts discussed in Chapter 3. It will give you a pattern to follow when answering questions at the end of the chapter in your text and for the problems that follow in this Study Guide.

   Suppose we have the following information about the productivity of industry in Japan and Korea. The data are the units of output per hour of work.

	steel	televisions
Japan	6	3
Korea	8	2

   A Japanese worker can produce 6 units of steel or 3 units of TVs per hour. A Korean worker can produce 8 units of steel or 2 units of TVs per hour.

   We can plot the production possibilities frontier for each country assuming each country has only one worker and the worker works only one hour. To plot the frontier, plot the end points and connect them with a line. For example, Japan can produce 6 units of steel with its worker or 3 units of televisions. It can also allocate one half hour to the production of each and get 3 units steel and 1-1/2 TVs. Any other proportion of the hour can be allocated to the two productive activities. The production possibilities frontier is linear in these cases because the labour resource can be moved from the production of one good to the other at a constant rate. We can do the same for Korea. Without trade, the production possibilities frontier is the consumption possibilities frontier, too.

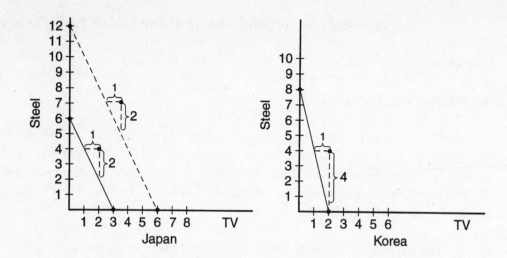

Comparative advantage determines specialization and trade. The opportunity cost of a TV in Japan is 2 units of steel, which is shown by the slope of the production possibilities frontier in the previous graph. Alternatively, the opportunity cost of one unit of steel in Japan is 1/2 of a TV. In Korea, the opportunity cost of a TV is 4 units of steel and the cost of a unit of steel is 1/4 of a TV. Since the opportunity cost of a TV is lower in Japan, Japan has a comparative advantage in TV production and should specialize in TVs. Since the opportunity cost of steel is lower in Korea, Korea has a comparative advantage in steel production and should specialize in steel.

What is the range of prices at which each country would be willing to exchange? If Japan specializes in TV production and produces 3 televisions, it would be willing to trade TVs for steel as long as the price of steel is below 1/2 a TV per unit of steel because that was the Japanese price for a unit of steel prior to trade. Korea would be willing to specialize in steel production and trade for TVs as long as the price of a TV is less than 4 units of steel because that was the Korean price of a TV prior to trade. In short, the final price must be between the original tradeoffs each faced in the absence of trade. One TV will cost between 2 and 4 of units of steel. One unit of steel will cost between 1/2 and 1/4 of a TV.

2. *Trade allows countries to consume outside their original production possibilities frontier.* Suppose that Japan and Korea settle on a trading price of 3 units of steel for 1 TV (or 1/3 of a TV for 1 unit of steel). (We are giving you this price. There is nothing in the problem that would let you calculate the final trading price. You can only calculate the range in which it must lie.) This price is halfway between the two prices that each faces in the absence of trade. The range for the trading price is 4 units of steel for 1 TV to 2 units of steel for 1 TV.

If Japan specializes in TV production, produces 3 televisions, and exports 1 TV for 3 units of steel, Japan will be able to consume 2 TVs and 3 units of steel. If we plot this point (2 TVs and 3 steel) on Japan's graph, we see that it lies outside its production possibilities frontier. If Korea specializes, produces 8 units of steel, and exports 3 units for 1 TV, Korea will be able to consume 5 units of steel and 1 TV. If we plot this point (5 steel and 1 TV) on Korea's graph, we see that it also lies outside its production possibilities frontier.

This is the gain from trade. Trade allows countries (and people) to specialize. Specialization increases world output. After trading, countries consume outside their individual production possibilities frontiers. In this way, trade is like an improvement in technology. It allows countries to move beyond their current production possibilities frontiers.

3. *Only comparative advantage matters — absolute advantage is irrelevant.* In the previous example, Japan had an absolute advantage in the production of TVs because it could produce 3 per hour while Korea could only produce 2. Korea had an absolute advantage in the production of steel because it could produce 8 units per hour compared to 6 for Japan.

To demonstrate that comparative advantage, not absolute advantage, determines specialization and trade, we alter the previous example so that Japan has an absolute advantage in the production of both goods. To this end, suppose Japan becomes twice as productive as in the previous table. That is, a worker can now produce 12 units of steel or 6 TVs per hour.

	steel	televisions
Japan	12	6
Korea	8	2

Now Japan has an absolute advantage in the production of both goods. Japan's new production possibilities frontier is the dashed line in the previous graph. Will this change the analysis? Not at all. The opportunity cost of each good within Japan is the same — 2 units of steel per TV or 1/2 TV per unit of steel (and Korea is unaffected). For this reason, Japan still has the identical comparative advantage as before and it will specialize in TV production while Korea will specialize in steel. However, since productivity has doubled in Japan, its entire set of choices has improved and, thus, its material welfare has improved.

II. Self-Testing Challenges

A. True/False Questions

_____1.   If Japan has an absolute advantage in the production of an item, it must also have a comparative advantage in the production of that item.

_____2.   Comparative advantage, not absolute advantage, determines the decision to specialize in production.

_____3.   Absolute advantage is a comparison based on productivity.

_____4.   Self-sufficiency is the best way to increase one's material welfare.

_____5.   Comparative advantage is a comparison based on opportunity cost.

_____6.   If a producer is self-sufficient, the production possibilities frontier is also the consumption possibilities frontier.

_____7.   If a country's workers can produce 5 hamburgers per hour or 10 bags of french fries per hour, absent trade, the price of 1 bag of fries is 2 hamburgers.

_____8.   If producers have different opportunity costs of production, trade will allow them to consume outside their production possibilities frontiers.

_____9.   If trade benefits one country, its trading partner must be worse off due to trade.

_____10. Talented people that are the best at everything have a comparative advantage in the production of everything.

_____11. The gains from trade can be measured by the increase in total production that comes from specialization.

_____12. When a country removes a specific import restriction, it always benefits every worker in that country.

_____13. If Germany's productivity doubles for everything it produces, this will not alter its prior pattern of specialization because it has not altered its comparative advantage.

_____14. If an advanced country has an absolute advantage in the production of everything, it will benefit if it eliminates trade with less developed countries and becomes completely self-sufficient.

_____15. If gains from trade are based solely on comparative advantage, and if all countries have the same opportunity costs of production, then there are no gains from trade.

B. Multiple-Choice Questions

1. If a nation has an absolute advantage in the production of a good,
    a. it can produce that good at a lower opportunity cost than its trading partner.
    b. it can produce that good using fewer resources than its trading partner.
    c. it can benefit by restricting imports of that good.
    d. it will specialize in the production of that good and export it.
    e. none of the above

2. If a nation has a comparative advantage in the production of a good,
    a. it can produce that good at a lower opportunity cost than its trading partner.
    b. it can produce that good using fewer resources than its trading partner.
    c. it can benefit by restricting imports of that good.
    d. it must be the only country with the ability to produce that good.
    e. none of the above

3. Which of the following statements about trade is true?
    a. Unrestricted international trade benefits every person in a country equally.
    b. People who are skilled at all activities cannot benefit from trade.

   c. Trade can benefit everyone in society because it allows people to specialize in activities in which they have an absolute advantage.

   d. Trade can benefit everyone in society because it allows people to specialize in activities in which they have a comparative advantage.

4. According to the principle of comparative advantage,

   a. countries with a comparative advantage in the production of every good need not specialize.

   b. countries should specialize in the production of goods that they enjoy consuming more than other countries.

   c. countries should specialize in the production of goods for which they use fewer resources in production than their trading partners.

   d. countries should specialize in the production of goods for which they have a lower opportunity cost of production than their trading partners.

5. Which of the following statements is true?

   a. Self-sufficiency is the road to prosperity for most countries.

   b. A self-sufficient country consumes outside its production possibilities frontier.

   c. A self-sufficient country can, at best, consume on its production possibilities frontier.

   d. Only countries with an absolute advantage in the production of every good should strive to be self-sufficient.

6. Suppose a country's workers can produce 4 watches per hour or 12 rings per hour. If there is no trade,

   a. the domestic price of 1 ring is 3 watches.

   b. the domestic price of 1 ring is 1/3 of a watch.

   c. the domestic price of 1 ring is 4 watches.

   d. the domestic price of 1 ring is 1/4 of a watch.

   e. the domestic price of 1 ring is 12 watches.

7. Suppose a country's workers can produce 4 watches per hour or 12 rings per hour. If there is no trade,

   a. the opportunity cost of 1 watch is 3 rings.

   b. the opportunity cost of 1 watch is 1/3 of a ring.

   c. the opportunity cost of 1 watch is 4 rings.

   d. the opportunity cost of 1 watch is 1/4 of a ring.

   e. the opportunity cost of 1 watch is 12 rings.

The following table shows the units of output a worker can produce per month in Australia and Korea. Use this table for questions 8-15.

	Food	Electronics
Australia	20	5
Korea	8	4

8. Which of the following statements about absolute advantage is true?
   a. Australia has an absolute advantage in the production of food while Korea has an absolute advantage in the production of electronics.
   b. Korea has an absolute advantage in the production of food while Australia has an absolute advantage in the production of electronics.
   c. Australia has an absolute advantage in the production of both food and electronics.
   d. Korea has an absolute advantage in the production of both food and electronics.

9. The opportunity cost of 1 unit of electronics in Australia is
   a. 5 units of food.
   b. 1/5 of a unit of food.
   c. 4 units of food.
   d. 1/4 of a unit of food.

10. The opportunity cost of 1 unit of electronics in Korea is
    a. 2 units of food.
    b. 1/2 of a unit of food.
    c. 4 units of food.
    d. 1/4 of a unit of food.

11. The opportunity cost of 1 unit of food in Australia is
    a. 5 units of electronics.
    b. 1/5 of a unit of electronics.
    c. 4 units of electronics.
    d. 1/4 of a unit of electronics.

12. The opportunity cost of 1 unit of food in Korea is
    a. 2 units of electronics.
    b. 1/2 of a unit of electronics.
    c. 4 units of electronics.
    d. 1/4 of a unit of electronics.

13. Which of the following statements about comparative advantage is true?
    a. Australia has a comparative advantage in the production of food while Korea has a comparative advantage in the production of electronics.
    b. Korea has a comparative advantage in the production of food while Australia has a comparative advantage in the production of electronics.
    c. Australia has a comparative advantage in the production of both food and electronics.
    d. Korea has a comparative advantage in the production of both food and electronics.
    e. There is no comparative advantage for either country because the opportunity cost of producing each good is the same in each country.

14. Korea should
   a. specialize in food production, export food, and import electronics.
   b. specialize in electronics production, export electronics, and import food.
   c. produce both goods because neither country has a comparative advantage.
   d. produce neither good because it has an absolute disadvantage in the production of both goods.

15. Prices of electronics can be stated in terms of units of food. What is the range of prices of electronics for which both countries could gain from trade?
   a. The price must be greater than 1/5 of a unit of food but less than 1/4 of a unit of food.
   b. The price must be greater than 4 units of food but less than 5 units of food.
   c. The price must be greater than 1/4 of a unit of food but less than 1/2 of a unit of food.
   d. The price must be greater than 2 units of food but less than 4 units of food.

16. Suppose the world consists of two countries — the U.S. and Canada. Further, suppose there are only two goods — food and clothing. Which of the following statements is true?
   a. If the U.S. has an absolute advantage in the production of food, then Canada must have an absolute advantage in the production of clothing.
   b. If the U.S. has a comparative advantage in the production of food, then Canada must have a comparative advantage in the production of clothing.
   c. If the U.S. has a comparative advantage in the production of food, it must also have a comparative advantage in the production of clothing.
   d. If the U.S. has a comparative advantage in the production of food, Canada might also have a comparative advantage in the production of food.
   e. None of the above.

Use the following production possibilities frontiers to answer questions 17-19. Assume each country has the same number of workers, say 20 million, and that each axis is measured in tonnes per month.

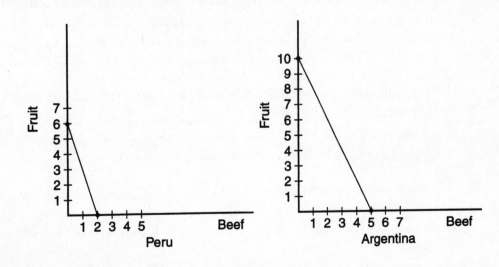

17. Argentina has a comparative advantage in the production of
    a. both fruit and beef.
    b. fruit.
    c. beef.
    d. neither fruit nor beef.

18. Peru will export
    a. both fruit and beef.
    b. fruit.
    c. beef.
    d. neither fruit nor beef.

19. The opportunity cost of producing a tonne of beef in Peru is
    a. 1/3 tonne of fruit.
    b. 1 tonne of fruit.
    c. 2 tonnes of fruit.
    d. 3 tonnes of fruit.
    e. 6 tonnes of fruit.

20. Joe is a tax accountant. He receives $100 per hour doing tax returns. He can type 10 000 characters per hour into spreadsheets. He can hire an assistant who types 2500 characters per hour into spreadsheets. Which of the following statements is true?
    a. Joe should not hire an assistant because the assistant cannot type as fast as he can.
    b. Joe should hire the assistant as long as he pays the assistant less than $100 per hour.
    c. Joe should hire the assistant as long as he pays the assistant less than $25 per hour.
    d. None of the above.

C. Short-Answer Questions

1. Why do people choose to become interdependent as opposed to self-sufficient?
   _____
   _____
   _____

2. Why is comparative advantage instead of absolute advantage important in determining trade? _____
   _____
   _____

3. What are the gains from trade?_____
   _____
   _____

4. Why is a restriction of trade likely to reduce material welfare? _____

_____

_____

_____

5. Suppose that a lawyer earning $200 per hour can also type at 200 words per minute. Should the lawyer hire a secretary who can only type 50 words per minute? Why? _____

_____

_____

6. Evaluate this statement: A technologically advanced country, which is better than its neighbour at producing everything, would be better off if it closed its borders to trade because the less productive country is a burden to the advanced country.

_____

_____

_____

_____

D. Practice Problems

1. Angela is a college student. She takes a full load of classes and has only 5 hours per week for her hobby. Angela is artistic and can make 2 clay pots per hour or 4 coffee mugs per hour.

   a. Draw Angela's production possibilities frontier for pots and mugs based on the amount produced per week.

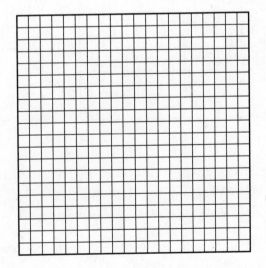

b. What is Angela's opportunity cost of one pot? 10 pots?_____
_____

c. What is Angela's opportunity cost of one mug? 10 mugs?_____
_____

d. Why is her production possibilities frontier a straight line instead of bowed out like those presented in Chapter 2?_____
_____

2. Suppose a worker in Germany can produce 15 computers or 5 tonnes of grain per month. Suppose a worker in Poland can produce 4 computers or 4 tonnes of grain per month. For simplicity, assume that each country has only one worker.

a. Fill out the following table:

	Computers	Grain
Germany		
Poland		

b. Graph the production possibilities frontier for each country.

c. What is the opportunity cost of a computer in Germany? What is the opportunity cost of a tonne of grain in Germany?_____
_____

d. What is the opportunity cost of a computer in Poland? What is the opportunity cost of a tonne of grain in Poland?_____
_____

e. Which country has the absolute advantage in producing computers? Grain?_____

f. Which country has the comparative advantage in producing computers? Grain?_____

g. Each country should tend toward specialization in the production of which good? Why?_____

h. What are the range of prices for computers and grain for which both countries would benefit?_____

i. Suppose Germany and Poland settle on a price of 2 computers for 1 tonne of grain or 1/2 tonne of grain for a computer. Suppose each country specializes in production and they trade 4 computers for 2 tonnes of grain. Plot the final consumption points on the graphs you made in part (b) above. Are these countries consuming inside or outside of their production possibilities frontier?_____

j. Suppose the productivity of a worker in Poland doubles so that a worker can produce 8 computers or 8 tonnes of grain per month. Which country has the absolute advantage in producing computers? Grain?_____

k. After the doubling of productivity in Poland, which country has a comparative advantage in producing computers? Grain? Has the comparative advantage changed? Has the material welfare of either country changed?_____

1. How would your analysis change if you assumed, more realistically, that each country had 10 million workers?_____

_____

_____

3. Suppose a worker in Canada can produce 4 cars or 20 computers per month while a worker in Russia can produce 1 car or 5 computers per month. Again, for simplicity, assume each country has only one worker.

    a. Fill out the following table:

	Cars	Computers
Canada		
Russia		

    b. Which country has the absolute advantage in the production of cars? Computers?_____

    _____

    _____

    c. Which country has the comparative advantage in the production of cars? Computers?_____

    _____

    _____

    _____

    d. Are there any gains to be made from trade? Why?_____

    _____

    _____

    e. Does your answer in (d) above help you pinpoint a source for gains from trade?_____

    _____

    _____

    f. What might make two countries have different opportunity costs of production? (Use your imagination. This was not directly discussed in Chapter 3.) _____

    _____

    _____

E. Advanced Critical Thinking

You are watching an election debate on television. A candidate says, "We need to stop the flow of foreign automobiles into our country. If we limit the importation of automobiles, our domestic auto production will rise and Canada will be better off."

1. Is it likely that Canada will be better off if it limits auto imports? Explain. _____
_____
_____

2. Will anyone in Canada be better off if it limits auto imports? Explain. _____
_____
_____

3. In the real world, does every person in the country gain when restrictions on imports are reduced? Explain. _____
_____
_____

III. Solutions

A. True/False Questions

1. F; absolute advantage compares the quantities of inputs used in production while comparative advantage compares the opportunity costs.
2. T
3. T
4. F; restricting trade eliminates gains from trade.
5. T
6. T
7. F; the price of 1 bag of fries is 1/2 of a hamburger.
8. T
9. F; voluntary trade benefits both traders.
10. F; a low opportunity cost of producing one good implies a high opportunity cost of producing the other good.
11. T
12. F; it may harm those involved in that industry.
13. T
14. F; voluntary trade benefits all traders.
15. T

B. Multiple-Choice Questions

1. b	6. b	11. d	16. b
2. a	7. a	12. b	17. c
3. d	8. c	13. a	18. b
4. d	9. c	14. b	19. d
5. c	10. a	15. d	20. c

C. Short-Answer Questions

1. Because a consumer gets a greater variety of goods at a much lower cost than he or she could produce by himself or herself. That is, there are gains from trade.

2. What is important in trade is how a country's costs without trade differ from each other. This is determined by the relative opportunity costs across countries.

3. The additional output that comes from countries with different opportunity costs of production specializing in the production of the item for which they have the lower domestic opportunity cost.

4. Because it forces people to produce at a higher cost than they pay when they trade.

5. Yes, as long as the secretary earns less than $50/hour, the lawyer is ahead.

6. This is not true. All countries can gain from trade if their opportunity costs of production differ. Even the least productive country will have a comparative advantage at producing something, and it can trade this good to the advanced country for less than the advanced country's opportunity cost.

D. Practice Problems

1. a.

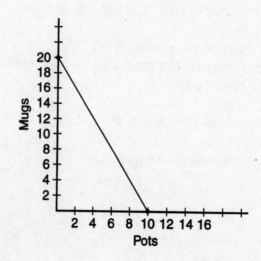

b. 2 mugs. 20 mugs.

c. 1/2 pot. 5 pots.

d. Because here resources can be moved from the production of one good to another at a constant rate.

2. a.

	Computers	Grain
Germany	15	5
Poland	4	4

b.

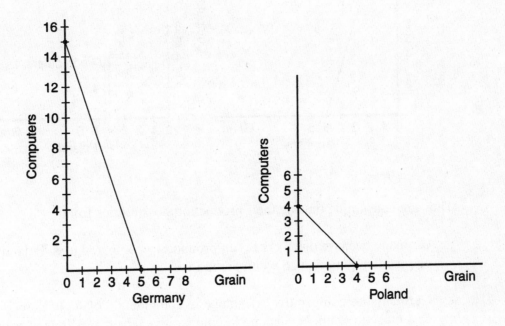

c. 1/3 tonne grain. 3 computers.

d. 1 tonne grain. 1 computer.

e. Germany because one worker can produce 15 compared to 4. Germany because one worker can produce 5 compared to 4.

f. Germany because a computer has the opportunity cost of only 1/3 tonne of grain compared to 1 tonne of grain in Poland. Poland because a tonne of grain has the opportunity cost of only 1 computer compared to 3 computers in Germany.

g. Germany should produce computers while Poland should produce grain because the opportunity cost of computers is lower in Germany and the opportunity cost of grain is lower in Poland. That is, each has a comparative advantage in those goods.

h. Grain must cost less than 3 computers to Germany. Computers must cost less than 1 tonne of grain to Poland.

i.

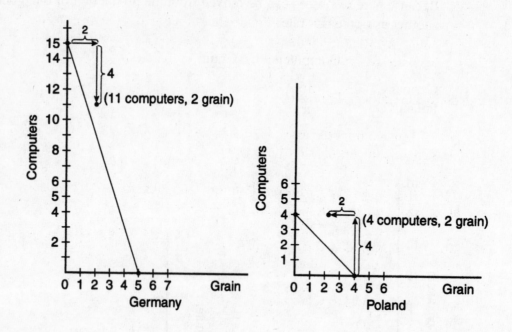

They are consuming outside their production possibilities frontier.

j. Germany because one worker can produce 15 compared to 8. Poland because one worker can produce 8 compared to 5.

k. Germany has comparative advantage in computers. Poland has comparative advantage in grain. No change in comparative advantage. Poland is better off, however, because it now has a larger set of choices.

l. It would not change absolute advantage or comparative advantage. It would change the scale in the previous two graphs by a factor of 10 million.

3. a.   Cars   Computers

    Canada   4   20
    Russia   1   5

b. Canada because one worker can produce 4 compared to 1. Canada because one worker can produce 20 compared to 5.

c. In both, the opportunity cost of 1 car is 5 computers. In both, the opportunity cost of 1 computer is 1/5 of a car. Therefore, neither has a comparative advantage in either good.

    d. No. Each can get the same tradeoff between goods domestically.

    e. Yes. There need to be differences in opportunity costs of producing goods across countries for there to be gains from trade.

    f. Resources or technology might be different across countries. That is, workers could be differently educated, land could be of different quality, or the available technology might be different.

E. Advanced Critical Thinking

1. No. If Canada imports autos, it is because the opportunity cost of producing them elsewhere is lower than in Canada.

2. Yes. Those associated with the domestic auto industry — stockholders of domestic auto producers and autoworkers.

3. No. When we reduce restrictions on imports, the country gains from the increased trade but individuals in the affected domestic industry may lose.

Chapter 4: The Market Forces of Supply and Demand

I. Chapter Overview

A. Context and Purpose

Earlier chapters provided an overview of the "economic way of thinking" in order to explain the operation of a mixed market economy such as that of Canada. One of the cornerstones of a market economy is the interaction of supply and demand. Unfortunately, these terms are not well understood: A parrot can be taught to squawk "supply and demand" without any knowledge of the concepts. You can read the newspapers on any given day and find examples of the misuse of supply and demand. The terms take on a very specific meaning in economics that differs from their everyday use. This chapter explains what an economist means by supply and demand and shows how they interact to determine prices and quantities of goods and services. It also shows how various factors that change either supply or demand ultimately lead to changes in market prices and quantities.

B. Helpful Hints

1. *Supply means willingness to sell.* In everyday usage, supply often refers to physical stocks of a product or resource in the form of inventories available for sale. In economics, however, **supply** means *willingness to sell*. For example, the newspapers often report changes in global petroleum supplies, when really they mean inventories or petroleum reserves. The supply of petroleum is the willingness to sell those reserves, not the petroleum itself.

2. *Demand means willingness to buy.* Demand is not simply consumer wants. Demand represents wants backed up by dollars and our willingness to spend them.

3. *A market is a collection of buyers and sellers.* Markets are not physical locations; rather they are the interaction of buyers and sellers. Such interaction **can** occur at a physical location: for example, an auction may represent a separate market. However, buyers and sellers can interact on a national or even global level, particularly as electronic communications grow. Money markets, for example, involve buyers and sellers around the world.

4. *"Demand" is the entire schedule or curve.* Demand refers to the whole demand schedule or demand curve, not just a point on the curve. It represents all of the price-quantity combinations that are acceptable to consumers. Because of this, we do not refer to increased sales due to a price cut as an increase in *demand*. There is, of course, an increase in the *quantity demanded*, but this is not an increase (or shift to the right) in demand itself.

NEL

5. *"Quantity Demanded" is a point on the demand curve.* When there is a change in price, quantity demanded changes, but demand itself does not change. Quantity demanded is synonymous with consumption, or sales, or quantity sold.

6. *"Supply" is the entire schedule or curve.* Supply refers to the whole supply schedule or supply curve, not just a point on the curve. For supply to shift, the underlying factors that we hold constant in plotting a supply curve must change. Changing the price simply means that we plot a new point on the existing supply curve, representing a new quantity. Of course an increase in price encourages suppliers to sell more; however, we call this response to higher price an increase in *quantity supplied*, rather than an increase (or shift) in *supply*.

7. *"Quantity Supplied" is a point on the supply curve.* When there is a change in price, the quantity supplied changes, even though the supply curve itself does not shift. The quantity supplied at a particular price is the amount that sellers are willing to sell at that price.

II. Self-Testing Challenges

A. True/False Questions

_____1.   A decrease in the price of soft drinks will increase their demand (shift the curve to the right).

_____2.   The supply of petroleum is fixed, because there is only a finite amount in the ground.

_____3.   At the equilibrium price, the amount that sellers are willing to provide is just equal to the amount that buyers are willing to buy.

_____4.   An improvement in technology tends to reduce the supply (shift it to the left).

_____5.   An increase in raw materials prices tends to reduce the supply (shift it to the left).

_____6.   If sellers expect prices to rise in the future, this could cause prices to rise today by encouraging sellers to reduce their current supply in anticipation of a price hike.

_____7.   A market refers to a physical location in which buyers and sellers interact.

_____8.   A price below equilibrium results in excess supply.

_____9.   Excess demand tends to drive price up until the market reaches equilibrium price and quantity.

_____10. An increase in supply tends to increase equilibrium price and quantity.

_____11. An equal increase in both supply and demand tends to increase equilibrium price and quantity.

_____12. An increase in supply accompanied by a proportionate decrease in demand tends to decrease equilibrium price while leaving equilibrium quantity unchanged.

_____13. The market supply curve is the vertical summation of all the individual supply curves.

_____14. Assuming that pizza and beer are complements, a decrease in the price of pizza would increase the demand for beer.

_____15. If pizza and hamburgers are substitutes, a decrease in the price of pizza would increase the demand for hamburgers.

B. Multiple-Choice Questions

1. Which of the following would not increase the demand (shift the curve to the right) for beer?
   a. A new Health Canada study concludes that beer cures colds and skin disorders.
   b. A price war results in beer selling for $.05/bottle.
   c. Bars begin giving away spicy snacks to their customers.
   d. The price of a substitute, hard liquor, rises.
   e. There is an increase in the drinking-age population.

2. If buyers believe that the price of automobile antifreeze will rise soon, due to an increase in the price of ethylene glycol which is used to make antifreeze, the most likely immediate result will be:
   a. a decrease (shift to the left) in the demand for antifreeze, due to a change in tastes.
   b. a decrease (shift to the left) in the demand for antifreeze, due to a shift to substitutes.
   c. an increase in the quantity demanded, due to the change in supply.
   d. an increase (shift to the right) in the demand for antifreeze, due to a change in expectations.
   e. no change in demand; only supply will change.

3. If a new technological breakthrough in genetic engineering makes it possible to grow twice as much corn per hectare as had been possible in the past, the most likely result will be:
   a. a decrease (shift to the left) in the supply of corn, due to the increased costs associated with the new technology.
   b. an increase (shift to the right) in the supply of corn, due to the reduced cost of production.
   c. an increase in the demand for corn, due to the greatly reduced price.
   d. an increase in quantity supplied, due to the increased willingness to sell corn.
   e. a shift from corn production to wheat production, using all of the extra land not needed for corn production.

4. A university student made the following statement to a friend at a university

sporting event: "This football stadium is a good example of how unrealistic economics is: my economics professor claims that according to a so-called 'Law of Supply,' supply varies directly with price, yet anybody can look around and see that the supply is fixed at 10 000 seats, no matter what the price is!" What was wrong with his statement?

a. This is simply an exception to the Law of Supply; it doesn't mean that it isn't relevant for most cases.

b. Supply isn't fixed at 10 000 seats; it is *quantity supplied* that is fixed.

c. Supply isn't the same thing as the physical stock of a good or service that is available; rather, supply is *willingness to sell*.

d. *Supply* doesn't vary directly with price, it is *quantity supplied* that varies with price.

e. Both c and d are correct.

Use the following graph to answer questions 5-8:

The Market for Personal Size Pizzas

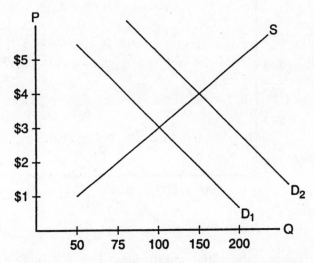

5. On the graph above, the initial equilibrium price and quantity are:
   a. P=$2.00; Q=75.
   b. P=$2.00; Q=150.
   c. P=$3.00; Q=100.
   d. P=$4.00; Q=75.
   e. P=$4.00; Q=150.

6. Which of the following would cause the demand for pizzas to shift to the right among university students?
   a. an increase in financial aid to university students
   b. half-price pizzas for anybody with a university ID
   c. an increase in the price of a complement, beer
   d. a decrease in the price of a substitute, hamburgers
   e. a drop in the number of students attending university

7. After an increase in demand, the new equilibrium price and quantity are:
   a. P=$2.00; Q=75.
   b. P=$2.00; Q=150.
   c. P=$3.00; Q=100.
   d. P=$4.00; Q=75.
   e. P=$4.00; Q=150.

8. The increase in demand would cause supply to:
   a. decrease (shift to the left).
   b. increase (shift to the right).
   c. first increase, then decrease over time.
   d. either rise or fall, depending on the magnitude of the change in demand.
   e. neither rise nor fall, although quantity supplied would increase.

Use the following graph to answer questions 9-12:

The Market for Hand-Held Calculators

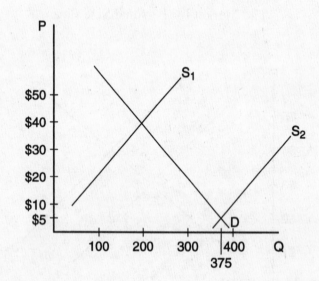

9. On the graph above, the initial equilibrium price and quantity are:
   a. P=$5; Q=375.
   b. P=$10; Q=350.
   c. P=$20; Q=100.
   d. P=$30; Q=250.
   e. P=$40; Q=200.

10. Of the following, the factor that would cause an increase (shift to the right) in supply is:
    a. improved technology.
    b. lower labour productivity.
    c. increased prices of substitutes.
    d. increased demand.
    e. higher price.

11. As a result of the increase in supply, the new equilibrium price and quantity are:
    a. P=$5; Q=375.
    b. P=$10; Q=350.
    c. P=$20; Q=100.
    d. P=$30; Q=250.
    e. P=$40; Q=200.

12. Suppose that the demand for calculators rose even more than the supply had increased. The net effect of the two increases would be the following change in equilibrium price and quantity:
    a. an increase in quantity but a slight decrease in price.
    b. increases in both quantity and price.
    c. decreases in both quantity and price.
    d. an increase in price but a decrease in quantity.
    e. an increase in price but an indeterminate effect on quantity.

13. Supply curves represent
    a. willingness to sell.
    b. physical stocks.
    c. inventories.
    d. willingness to buy.
    e. total production.

14. The supply curve for a good or service shows the sellers'
    a. target price.
    b. minimum acceptable price.
    c. maximum acceptable price.
    d. average acceptable price.
    e. inventories of finished products.

15. If equilibrium quantity rises but equilibrium price remains unchanged, the cause is:
    a. an increase in both supply and demand.
    b. an increase in demand and decrease in supply.
    c. a decrease in demand and increase in supply.
    d. a decrease in both demand and supply.
    e. an increase in demand in a market subject to a price ceiling.

16. If equilibrium price rises but equilibrium quantity remains unchanged, the cause is:
    a. an increase in both supply and demand.
    b. an increase in demand and decrease in supply.
    c. a decrease in demand and increase in supply.
    d. a decrease in both demand and supply.
    e. an increase in demand in a market subject to a price ceiling.

17. If equilibrium quantity and price rise, the cause is:
    a. an increase in demand without a change in supply.
    b. an increase in demand and decrease in supply.
    c. a decrease in demand and increase in supply.
    d. a decrease in both demand and supply.
    e. an increase in demand in a market subject to a price ceiling.

18. A freeze that destroys half of the coffee crop in South America would likely raise the price of coffee,
    a. reducing the demand for coffee and increasing the demand for tea.
    b. reducing the quantity demanded for coffee and increasing the demand for tea.
    c. reducing the demand for both coffee and tea.
    d. reducing the quantity demanded for both coffee and tea.
    e. reducing the demand for coffee and increasing the supply of coffee.

19. An inferior good is one for which demand:
    a. rises as income rises.
    b. falls as income rises.
    c. is unrelated to income.
    d. is low because of the low quality of the good.
    e. is high because the good must be replaced often.

20. Suppose that there is a shortage of parking spaces in downtown Toronto during weekdays. The shortage can be eliminated by
    a. government lowering the price.
    b. increasing the quantity demanded.
    c. allowing the price to rise.
    d. decreasing the supply.
    e. in this particular market, the shortage cannot be eliminated.

C. Short-Answer Questions

1. What would happen to the demand for apples if consumers' income rose, and apples are a normal good? What if apples are an inferior good? Explain briefly.

    _____

    _____

    _____

    _____

2. Explain why the price of a complement or a substitute can alter the demand for a good, even though the price of the good itself does not shift the demand.

    _____

    _____

    _____

D. Practice Problems

The supply and demand schedules below show hypothetical prices and quantities in the market for corn. The initial quantity supplied is shown by Q_s, and the quantity demanded is Q_d.

The Market for Corn
(in millions of tonnes)

Price	Q_d	Q_s	$Q_{s'}$
$6.00	220	400	____
$5.50	240	360	____
$5.00	260	320	____
$4.50	280	280	____
$4.00	300	240	____
$3.50	320	200	____
$3.00	340	160	____

1. Plot the supply and demand curves for the initial supply and demand, Q_s and Q_d on the graph that follows the questions.

   a. The equilibrium price of corn is $_____.

   b. The equilibrium quantity of corn is _____ million tonnes.

   c. At a price of $3.00/tonne, there would be a (shortage, surplus) _____ of _____ million tonnes, and the price would tend to (fall, rise) _____.

   d. At a price of $5.00/tonne, there would be a (shortage, surplus) _____ of _____ million tonnes, and the price would tend to (fall, rise) _____.

2. Suppose that the supply of corn increased by 60 million tonnes at every price. Show the new supply schedule as $Q_{s'}$ on the previous table.

   a. The new equilibrium price of corn is $_____.

   b. The new equilibrium quantity of corn is _____ million tonnes.

   c. Has the demand for corn changed as a result of this change in supply? Explain briefly. _____

   _____

   _____

3. Give an example of a factor that could have caused such an increase in the supply of corn, and explain briefly. _____

   _____

   _____

4. Notice that the increase in supply has resulted in a lower price and a higher quantity. Does this violate the Law of Supply, which states that the quantity of a good supplied increases as its price increases, all else equal? Explain briefly.

_____

_____

_____

The Market for Corn

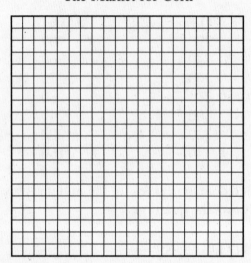

E. Advanced Critical Thinking

Consider the following editorial that appeared in a leading U.S. business publication, following a freeze that destroyed much of the coffee crop in the late 1970s:

> *Coffee prices, it seems, are coming down again, after hitting a record high of $4.42 last year. An Agriculture Department economist, who had predicted $5-a-pound coffee this year, says he "underestimated the power of the U.S. consumer movement." Perhaps, or maybe, as with so many economists these days, he simply forgot his freshman economics, which has nothing to do with "movements." The coffee market is behaving the way the basic textbooks say a market behaves: Prices go up, demand falls, and prices come down.*
> *— The Wall Street Journal, November 30, 1977*

1. Suppose that coffee had started out at an equilibrium price of $1.00/pound prior to the freeze.

    a. Show graphically the initial equilibrium, labelling supply and demand as S_1 and D_1, respectively. Use Q_1 to identify the original equilibrium quantity.

    b. Show graphically the effect of a freeze that destroys much of the coffee crop, labelling the new supply as S_2 and the new equilibrium quantity as Q_2. (The new equilibrium price is $4.42.)

   c. Did you show a change in demand in your answer to part (b)? Why or why not?

_____

_____

   d. Based on your analysis in parts (a-c), critique the *Wall Street Journal* editorial. What's wrong with their analysis? _____

_____

_____

_____

III. Solutions

A. True/False Questions

1. F; quantity demanded, not demand, will increase.
2. F; the physical stock of petroleum in the ground is fixed, but the supply is willingness to sell, which is not fixed.
3. T
4. F; technology tends to *increase* the supply (shift it to the right) by increasing productivity; that is, increasing output per unit of input.
5. T
6. T
7. F; a market need not be in a specific physical location; buyers and sellers can interact without being in the same location.
8. F; price below equilibrium results in excess demand, as buyers try to buy more than sellers are willing to sell at the low price.
9. T
10. F; increased supply moves the equilibrium to the right along the demand curve, resulting in a higher quantity and lower price.
11. F; an increase in both supply and demand will increase equilibrium quantity, but the effect on price depends on which curve shifts more; if they shift equally, price remains unchanged.
12. T
13. F; market supply is the horizontal summation of the individual supply curves; for each price, it represents the sum of all of the individual quantities supplied.
14. T
15. F; a decrease in the price of a good tends to decrease the demand for its substitutes.

B. Multiple-Choice Questions

1. b	6. a	11. a	16. b
2. d	7. e	12. b	17. a
3. b	8. e	13. a	18. b
4. e	9. e	14. b	19. b
5. c	10. a	15. a	20. c

C. Short-Answer Questions

1. An increase in consumer income increases the demand for normal goods and decreases the demand for inferior goods. This result would hold for apples just as it does for other goods.

2. Prices of other goods are held constant in deriving a demand curve, even though they can affect consumption. When they change, the demand also changes (shifts right or left). The price of the good itself does not shift the demand, however, because price is already built into our definition of demand. Demand for a good includes all of the quantities that consumers are willing to buy at various prices of the good, holding other factors constant.

D. Practice Problems

1. a. $4.50

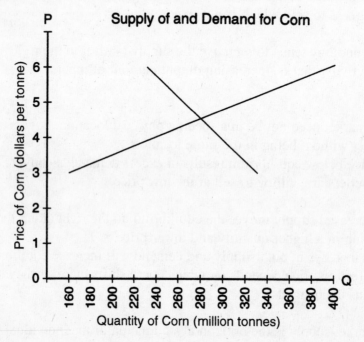

b. 280

c. shortage, 180, rise

d. surplus, 60, fall

2. a. $4.00

b. 300

c. Demand has not changed. Supply increased, moving the equilibrium along the existing demand curve to a higher quantity and lower price.

3. Any of the factors that lower cost of production could shift the supply to the right, indicating increased willingness to sell at each price. For example, improvements in technology that increase productivity would lower cost and increase the supply.

4. No, this does not violate the Law of Supply. The Law of Supply holds other factors, such as technology, constant. This represents a new supply curve, with an increased *willingness to sell*, corresponding to increased productivity. Both the old and new supply curves follow the Law of Supply: as long as those other factors are constant, sellers will tend to be willing to sell more only at a higher price.

E. Advanced Critical Thinking

1. a. The original equilibrium should be at a price of $1.00, with the quantity simply labelled Q_1.

   b. The new equilibrium should be at a price of $4.42 and a quantity of Q_2, after a leftward shift in supply and a movement along the (unchanged) demand curve. Equilibrium price is higher and quantity is lower.

   c. Demand did not change; only the quantity demanded changed as the supply shifted left, moving along the existing demand curve. There were no changes in the factors that are held constant in deriving a demand curve.

   d. The newspaper's analysis was flawed. They confused (shifts in) demand with simple changes in quantity demanded in response to a price change. For the price to fall, one of the factors (other than price) affecting either supply or demand must have changed.

Chapter 5: Measuring a Nation's Income

I. Chapter Overview

A. Context and Purpose

Chapter 5 is the first chapter in the macroeconomic section of the text. It is the first of a two-chapter sequence that introduces you to two vital statistics that economists use to monitor the macroeconomy — GDP and the consumer price index. Chapter 5 develops how economists measure production and income in the macroeconomy. The following chapter, Chapter 6, develops how economists measure the level of prices in the macroeconomy. Taken together, Chapter 5 concentrates on the *quantity* of output in the macroeconomy while Chapter 6 addresses *prices* in the macroeconomy.

The purpose of this chapter is to provide you with an understanding of the measurement and use of gross domestic product (GDP). GDP is the single most important measure of the health of the macroeconomy. Indeed, it is the most widely reported statistic in every developed economy.

B. Helpful Hints

1. *GDP measures production.* When we set out to measure GDP, we must first remember that we are measuring *production* over a period of time. If we can remember that, we will generally account for unusual types of production correctly. Examples:

   - How should we handle the measurement of the production of a cruise ship that takes three years to build and is sold at the end of the third year? Logically, we should count the portion of the ship that was completed during each year and apply it to that year's GDP. In fact, that is what economists do. If we had accounted for the entire ship in the year in which it was sold, we would have overestimated GDP in the third year and underestimated GDP in the previous two years.

   - Similarly, if a new house was built during one year but sold for the first time during the next year, we should account for it during the first year because that is when it was produced. That is, the builder "purchased" the finished home during the first year and added it to his or her inventory of homes.

   While in general we only wish to count final goods and services, we do count the production of intermediate goods that were not used during the period but were added to a firm's inventory because this production will not be captured by counting all of the final goods.

2. *GDP does not include all expenditures.* We have learned that we can measure GDP by adding the expenditures on final goods and services ($Y = C + I + G + NX$). Once we have learned the expenditure approach, however, we must not forget the words "on final goods and services" and mistakenly count all expenditures. When we include expenditures on used items, intermediate goods, stocks and bonds, or government transfer payments, we get a very large dollar value, but it has nothing to do with GDP. The dollar value of total transactions in the economy is enormous and many times that of GDP.

3. *Intermediate goods and final goods are distinct.* It should be helpful to clarify the distinction between intermediate goods and final goods with an example. Recall:

   • Intermediate goods are goods that are produced by one firm to be further processed by another firm.

   • Final goods are sold to the end user.

   GDP only includes the value of the final goods and services because the value of the intermediate goods used in the production of a final good or service is fully captured in the price of the final good or service. If we include the value of intermediate production in GDP, we would double count the intermediate goods.

   If we understand this distinction, can we list the *items* in the economy that are intermediate or final? For example, is a tire an intermediate good or a final good? The answer is: it depends on who bought it. When General Motors buys a tire from Goodyear, the tire is an intermediate good because General Motors will attach it to a car and sell it. When you buy a tire from your Goodyear dealer, it is a final good and should be counted in GDP. Thus, it is difficult to list items in the economy that are intermediate or final without knowledge of the buyer.

4. *Comparisons of GDP across countries and time can be biased.* We should be cautious when we compare GDP across nations of different levels of market development and when we compare GDP across long periods of time within a single nation. This is because GDP excludes most non-market activities. Clearly, a greater proportion of the output of lesser developed nations is likely to be household production such as when someone does their own farming, cleaning, sewing, and maybe even home construction. Since these activities are not captured by a market transaction, they are not recorded in lesser developed nations or in earlier periods of industrialized nations when market development was less extensive. This results in an even lower estimate of their GDP.

II. Self-Testing Challenges

A. True/False Questions

_____1.   For an economy as a whole, income equals expenditure because the income of the seller must be equal to the expenditure of the buyer.

_____2.   The production of an apple contributes more to GDP than the production of a gold ring because food is necessary for life itself.

_____3.   If the lumber yard sells $1000 of lumber to a carpenter and the carpenter uses the lumber to build a garage that he sells for $5000, the contribution to GDP is $6000.

_____4.   A country with a larger GDP per person generally has a greater standard of living or quality of life than a country with a smaller GDP per person.

_____5.   If nominal GDP in 1997 exceeds nominal GDP in 1996, real output must have risen.

_____6.   When a Canadian citizen works temporarily in the United States, her production is part of U.S. GDP.

_____7.   Wages are an example of a transfer payment because there is a transfer of payment from the firm to the worker.

_____8.   In Canada, investment is the largest component of GDP.

_____9.   Nominal GDP employs current prices to value output while real GDP employs constant base-year prices to value output.

_____10. A new car produced in 1996, but first sold in 1997, should be counted in 1997 GDP because that is when it was first sold as a final good.

_____11. When the city of Halifax purchases a new hockey arena, the investment component of GDP increases.

_____12. A recession occurs when real GDP declines.

_____13. Depreciation is the value of the wear and tear on the economy's equipment and structures.

_____14. Cigarettes should be valued in GDP at $4.50 per pack even though $1.00 of that price is tax because the buyers paid $4.50 per pack.

_____15. Net exports equal exports plus imports.

B. Multiple-Choice Questions

1. An example of a transfer payment is
   a. wages.
   b. profit.
   c. rent.
   d. government purchases.
   e. employment insurance benefits.

2. The purchase of plant and equipment by General Motors is part of
   a. consumption.
   b. depreciation.
   c. exports.
   d. investment.
   e. intermediate production.

3. Which of the following would be excluded from 1989 GDP? The sale of
   a. a 1989 Chrysler made in Windsor, Ontario.
   b. a hair-cut.
   c. a realtor's services.
   d. a home built in 1988 and first sold in 1989.
   e. all of the above should be counted in 1989 GDP.

4. Gross Domestic Product can be measured as the sum of
   a. consumption, investment, government purchases, and net exports.
   b. consumption, transfer payments, wages, and profits.
   c. investment, wages, profits, and intermediate production.
   d. final goods and services, intermediate goods, transfer payments, and rent.
   e. Net National Product, Gross National Product, and disposable personal income.

5. Canadian Gross Domestic Product measures the production and income of
   a. Canadians and their factories no matter where they are located in the world.
   b. people and factories located within the borders of Canada.
   c. the domestic service sector only.
   d. the domestic manufacturing sector only.
   e. none of the above.

6. Gross Domestic Product is the sum of the market value of the
   a. intermediate goods.
   b. manufactured goods.
   c. normal goods and services.
   d. inferior goods and services.
   e. final goods and services.

7. If nominal GDP in 1998 exceeds nominal GDP in 1997, then the production of output must have
    a. risen.
    b. fallen.
    c. stayed the same.
    d. risen or fallen because there is not enough information to determine what happened to real output.

8. If a cobbler buys leather for $100 and thread for $50 and uses them to produce and sell $500 worth of shoes to consumers, the contribution to GDP is
    a. $50.
    b. $100.
    c. $500.
    d. $600.
    e. $650.

9. GDP would include which of the following?
    a. housework
    b. illegal drug sales
    c. intermediate sales
    d. consulting services
    e. the value of taking a day off from work

10. Real GDP is measured in _____ prices, while nominal GDP is measured in _____ prices.
    a. current year, base year
    b. base year, current year
    c. intermediate, final
    d. domestic, foreign
    e. foreign, domestic

The following table contains information about an economy that produces only pens and books. The base year is 1996. Use this information for questions 11-16.

Year	Price of Pens	Quantity of Pens	Price of Books	Quantity of Books
1996	$3	100	$10	50
1997	$3	120	$12	70
1998	$4	120	$14	70

11. What is the value of nominal GDP for 1997?
    a. $800
    b. $1060
    c. $1200
    d. $1460
    e. none of the above

12. What is the value of real GDP for 1997?
    a. $800
    b. $1060
    c. $1200
    d. $1460
    e. none of the above

13. What is the value of the GDP deflator in 1997?
    a. 100
    b. 113
    c. 116
    d. 119
    e. 138

14. What is the percentage increase in prices from 1996 to 1997?
    a. 0%
    b. 13%
    c. 16%
    d. 22%
    e. 38%

15. What is the approximate percentage increase in prices from 1997 to 1998?
    a. 0%
    b. 13%
    c. 16%
    d. 22%
    e. 38%

16. What is the percentage increase in real GDP from 1997 to 1998?
    a. 0%
    b. 7%
    c. 22%
    d. 27%
    e. 32%

17. GDP excludes which of the following?
    a. leisure
    b. value of goods and services produced at home
    c. volunteer work
    d. quality of the environment
    e. all of the above

18. Canadian GDP would exclude which of the following?
    a. lawyer services purchased by a homebuyer
    b. lawn care services purchased by a homeowner
    c. a new bridge purchased by the province of Prince Edward Island
    d. grapes purchased by a Niagara winery
    e. the purchase of a new Toyota car produced in Ontario

19. How is your purchase of a $60 000 BMW that was produced in Germany recorded in the Canadian GDP accounts?
    a. Investment increases by $60 000 and net exports increase by $60 000.
    b. Consumption increases by $60 000 and net exports decrease by $60 000.
    c. Net exports decrease by $60 000.
    d. Net exports increase by $60 000.

20. If your grandparents buy a new retirement home, this transaction would affect
    a. consumption.
    b. investment.
    c. government purchases.
    d. net exports.
    e. none of the above.

C. Short-Answer Questions

1. Why does income = expenditure = GDP? _____
    _____

2. Define GDP and explain the important terms in the definition.
    _____
    _____
    _____
    _____
    _____

3. What are the components of expenditure? Provide an example of each. _____
    _____
    _____
    _____

4. Provide an example of a transfer payment. Do we include it in GDP? Why? _____
    _____
    _____

5. If nominal GDP in 1998 exceeds nominal GDP in 1997, did real output rise? Did prices rise? _____
    _____

6. If real GDP in 1998 exceeds real GDP in 1997, did real output rise? Did prices rise?

_____

_____

_____

7. If you buy a $25 000 Toyota that was fully produced in Japan, does this affect
    Canadian GDP? Show how this transaction would affect the appropriate expenditure
    categories that make up GDP. _____

_____

_____

_____

8. In the year 2000, what was the approximate value of GDP per person? What
    component of GDP is the largest? _____

_____

_____

9. Which contributes more when measuring GDP, a new diamond necklace purchased
    by a wealthy person or a soft drink purchased by a thirsty person? Why? _____

_____

_____

10. If your neighbour hires you to mow her lawn instead of doing it herself, what will
    happen to GDP? Why? Did output change? _____

_____

_____

D. Practice Problems

1. a. Complete the following table.

	Year 1	Year 2	Year 3
Gross Domestic Product	4532	4804	
Consumption		3320	3544
Investment	589	629	673
Government Purchases	861		977
Net Exports	–45	–58	–54

b. What is the largest expenditure component of GDP? _____

_____

_____

c. Does investment include the purchase of stocks and bonds? Why? _____

_____

_____

_____

d. Does government purchases include government spending on Employment Insurance benefits? Why?_____

_____

e. What does it mean to say that net exports are negative? _____

_____

2. Suppose the base year in the following table is 1995.

Year	Production of X	Price per unit of X
1995	20 units	$ 5
1996	20 units	$10
1997	20 units	$20

a. What is nominal GDP for 1995, 1996, and 1997? _____

_____

b. What is real GDP for 1995, 1996, and 1997? _____

_____

3. Suppose the following table records the total output and prices for an entire economy. Further, suppose the base year in the following table is 1996.

Year	Price of soft drink	Quantity of soft drink	Price of jeans	Quantity of jeans
1996	$1.00	200	$10.00	50
1997	$1.00	220	$11.00	50

a. What is the value of nominal GDP in 1996? _____

b. What is the value of real GDP in 1996? _____

c. What is the value of nominal GDP in 1997? _____

d. What is the value of real GDP in 1997? _____

e. What is the value of the GDP deflator in 1996? _____

f. What is the value of the GDP deflator in 1997? _____

g. From 1996 to 1997, prices rose approximately what percentage? _____

h. Was the increase in nominal GDP from 1996 to 1997 mostly due to an increase in real output or due to an increase in prices? _____

_____

_____

4. Complete the following table.

Year	Nominal GDP	Real GDP	GDP deflator
1		$100	100
2	$120		120
3	$150	$125	

a. What year is the base year? How can you tell? _____
   _____
   _____

b. From year 1 to year 2, did real output rise or did prices rise? Explain.
   _____
   _____

c. From year 2 to year 3, did real output rise or did prices rise? Explain.
   _____
   _____

E. Advanced Critical Thinking

You are watching a news report with your father. The news anchor points out that a certain troubled Caribbean nation generates a GDP per person of only $340 (Canadian) per year. Since your father knows Canadian GDP per person is approximately $34 000, he suggests that we are materially 100 times better off in Canada than in the Caribbean nation.

1. Is your father's statement accurate? _____

2. What general category of production is not captured by GDP in both Canada and the Caribbean nation? _____
   _____

3. Provide some examples of this type of activity. _____
   _____
   _____

4. Why would the exclusion of this type of production affect the measurement of Caribbean output more than Canadian output? _____
   _____
   _____

5. Does this mean that residents of the Caribbean nation are actually as well off materially as residents in Canada? _____
   _____
   _____

III. Solutions

A. True/False Questions

1. T
2. F; contribution is based on market value.
3. F; the garage is the final good, valued at $5000.
4. T
5. F; prices or real output could have risen.
6. T
7. F; transfer payments are expenditures for which no good or service is received in return.
8. F; consumption is the largest component of GDP.
9. T
10. F; goods are counted in the year produced.
11. F; the purchase is included in government purchases.
12. T
13. T
14. T
15. F; $NX = X - M$.

B. Multiple-Choice Questions

1. e	6. e	11. c	16. a
2. d	7. d	12. b	17. e
3. d	8. c	13. b	18. d
4. a	9. d	14. b	19. b
5. b	10. b	15. d	20. b

C. Short-Answer Questions

1. Because the income of the seller equals the expenditure of the buyer and GDP can be measured with either one.

2. Market value of all final goods and services produced within a country in a given period of time. "Market value" – price paid, "of all" – all legal production, "final" – to end users, "goods and services" – includes services, "produced" – no used items, "within a country" – inside borders, "in a given period" – per quarter or year.

3. Consumption (food), investment (factory), government purchases (military equipment), net exports (sale of wheat to Japan minus purchase of wine from Germany).

4. Social assistance payments. No, because the government received no good or service in return.

5. We can't be certain which rose, prices or real output, because an increase in either prices or real output will cause nominal output to rise.

6. Real output rose because the value of output in each year is measured in constant base year prices. We have no information on prices.

7. No. Consumption would increase by $25 000 and net exports would decrease by $25 000. As a result, Canadian GDP is unaffected.

8. GDP per person, or the amount of expenditure for the averge Canadian, was about $34 000 per year. Consumption made up about 57 percent of GDP, or about $19 000 per person.

9. A diamond necklace because GDP measures market value.

10. GDP will rise because the mowing of the lawn was a market transaction. However, output didn't really rise.

D. Practice Problems

1. a.

	Year 1	Year 2	Year 3
Gross Domestic Product	4532	4804	5140
Consumption	3127	3320	3544
Investment	589	629	673
Government Purchases	861	913	977
Net Exports	–45	–58	–54

 b. consumption

 c. No, because that transaction is a purchase of an asset, not a purchase of currently produced capital goods.

 d. No, because Employment Insurance benefits are expenditures for which the government receives no production in return.

 e. It means that imports exceed exports.

2. a. $100, $200, $400

 b. $100, $100, $100

3. a. $700

    b. $700

    c. $770

    d. $720

    e. 100

    f. 107

    g. $(107 - 100)/100 = 0.07 = 7\%$

    h. Percent increase in nominal $(\$770 - \$700)/700 = 0.10 = 10\%$.
        Percent increase in prices $= 7\%$, therefore, most of the increase was due to prices.

4. | Year | Nominal GDP | Real GDP | GDP deflator |
    |------|-------------|----------|--------------|
    | 1 | $100 | $100 | 100 |
    | 2 | $120 | $100 | 120 |
    | 3 | $150 | $125 | 120 |

    a. Year 1, because the deflator $= 100$.

    b. Prices rose 20% and real output stayed the same.

    c. Prices stayed the same and real output rose 25%.

E. Advanced Critical Thinking

1. No.

2. Non-market activities.

3. Household production done by an individual without pay such as gardening, cleaning, sewing, home improvement or construction, child supervision, etc.

4. A greater proportion of the output produced by lesser developed nations is non-market output. That is, it is not sold and recorded as a market transaction.

5. No. It just means that quantitative comparisons between nations of greatly different levels of development are very difficult and often inaccurate.

Chapter 6: Measuring the Cost of Living

I. Chapter Overview

A. Context and Purpose

Chapter 6 is the second chapter of a two-chapter sequence that deals with how economists measure output and prices in the macroeconomy. Chapter 5 addressed how economists measure output. Chapter 6 develops how economists measure the overall price level in the macroeconomy.

The purpose of Chapter 6 is twofold: first, to show you how to generate a price index, and second, to teach you how to employ a price index to compare dollar figures from different points in time and to adjust interest rates for inflation. In addition, you will learn some of the shortcomings of using the consumer price index as a measure of the cost of living.

B. Helpful Hints

1. *The year we choose to determine the typical consumption basket must also be chosen as the base year.* When we construct the CPI, we choose a year to survey consumers and *fix the basket*. The year we choose to fix the basket must also be chosen as the base year. That is, we also use that year as the benchmark year against which other years are to be compared.

2. *Your particular consumption basket may not be typical.* Since the GDP deflator and the CPI are based on different baskets of goods and services, each will provide a slightly different measurement of the cost of living. Continuing in this same line of thinking, your particular consumption basket may differ from the typical consumption basket used by Statistics Canada when they calculate the CPI. For example, when you are a young adult, your basket may be more heavily weighted toward electronics and clothing. If clothing prices are rising faster than average, young people may have a greater increase in the cost of living than is suggested by the CPI. In like manner, when you become old, your consumption basket may be more heavily weighted toward home-care medical services and travel. Exceptional increases in these prices may cause the cost of living for the elderly to rise more quickly than suggested by the CPI.

3. *Dollar values can be adjusted backward in time as well as forward.* For example, suppose your mother earned an income of $20 000 in 1980 and $36 000 in 2000.

The CPI in 1980 (base year 1992) was 52.4 and the CPI in 2000 was 113.5. We can convert her 1980 salary into 2000 dollars as follows:

$$\$20\,000 \times (113.5/52.4) = \$43\,320.$$

Her $20 000 salary in 1980 would buy as much as a $43 320 salary in 2000. Since your mother earned $36 000 in 2000, her real income and standard of living fell over those 20 years.

Alternatively, we can convert her 2000 salary into 1980 dollars as follows:

$$\$36\,000 \times (52.4/113.5) = \$16\,620.$$

Her $36 000 salary in 2000 would buy as much as a $16 620 salary in 1980. Since your mother earned $20 000 in 1980, her real income and standard of living were higher in 1980.

4. *When correcting interest rates for inflation, think like a lender.* If you loan someone $100 for one year, and you charge them 7% interest, you will receive $107 at the end of the year. Did you receive 7 additional dollars of purchasing power? Suppose inflation was 4%. You would need to receive $104 at the end of the year just to break even. That is, you would need $104 just to be able to buy the same set of goods and services that you could have purchased for $100 at the time you granted the loan. In this sense, you received only 3 additional dollars of purchasing power for having made the $100 loan, or a 3% real return. Thus, the *real interest rate* on the loan is 3%. Using your formula:

$$7\% - 4\% = 3\%$$

Although not explicitly stated, the interest rate example in your text is also approached from the lender's perspective. That is, when you deposit money in a bank and receive interest, the deposit is actually a loan from you to the bank.

II. Self-Testing Challenges

A. True/False Questions

_____1.   An increase in the price of imported cameras is captured by the CPI but not by the GDP deflator.

_____2.   An increase in the price of helicopters purchased by the Canadian military is captured by the CPI.

_____3.   Because an increase in gasoline prices causes consumers to ride their bikes more and drive their cars less, the CPI tends to underestimate the cost of living.

_____4.   An increase in the price of diamonds will have a greater impact on the CPI than an equal percentage increase in the price of food because diamonds are so much more expensive.

_____5.   The "base year" in a price index is the benchmark year against which other years are compared.

_____6. If the CPI rises at 5% per year, then every individual in the country needs exactly a 5% increase in their income for their standard of living to remain constant.

_____7. The industrial product price index is constructed to measure the change in price of total production.

_____8. If Statistics Canada fails to recognize that recently produced automobiles can be driven for many more kilometres than older models, then the CPI tends to overestimate the cost of living.

_____9. If your wage rises from $6.00 to $7.25 while the CPI rises from 112 to 121, you should feel an increase in your standard of living.

_____10. The largest category of goods and services in the CPI is transportation.

_____11. It is impossible for *real* interest rates to be negative.

_____12. If the nominal interest rate is 12% and the rate of inflation is 7%, then the real rate of interest is 5%.

_____13. If lenders demand a real rate of return of 4% and they expect inflation to be 5%, then they should charge 9% interest when they extend loans.

_____14. If borrowers and lenders agree on a nominal interest rate and inflation turns out to be greater than they had anticipated, lenders will gain at the expense of borrowers.

_____15. If workers and firms agree on an increase in wages based on their expectations of inflation and inflation turns out to be less than they expected, workers will gain at the expense of firms.

B. Multiple-Choice Questions

1. Inflation can be measured by all of the following *except* the
    a. GDP deflator.
    b. consumer price index.
    c. industrial product price index.
    d. finished goods price index.
    e. all of the above are used to measure inflation.

2. The CPI will be most influenced by a 10% increase in the price of which of the following consumption categories?
    a. shelter
    b. transportation
    c. health and personal care
    d. food
    e. All of the above would produce the same impact.

3. In 1989, the CPI was 89.0. In 1990, it was 93.3. What was the rate of inflation for 1990?
   a. 3.1%
   b. 4.8%
   c. 6.7%
   d. 30.7%
   e. You can't tell without knowing the base year.

4. Which of the following would cause the CPI to rise more than the GDP deflator?
   a. an increase in the price of tanks purchased by the military
   b. an increase in the price of domestically produced telecommunications equipment sold exclusively to the United States
   c. an increase in the price of Hondas produced in Japan and sold in Canada
   d. an increase in the price of agricultural machinery

5. The "basket" on which the CPI is based is composed of
   a. raw materials purchased by firms.
   b. total current production.
   c. products purchased by the typical consumer.
   d. consumer production.
   e. none of the above.

6. If there is an increase in the price of apples that causes consumers to purchase fewer kilograms of apples and more kilograms of oranges, the CPI will suffer from
   a. substitution bias.
   b. bias due to the introduction of new goods.
   c. bias due to unmeasured quality change.
   d. base-year bias.
   e. none of the above.

Use the following table for questions 7 through 12. The table shows the prices and the quantities consumed in Carnivore Country. The base year is 1997. (This is also the year the typical consumption basket was determined.)

Year	Price of beef	Quantity of beef	Price of pork	Quantity of pork
1997	$2.00	100	$1.00	100
1998	$2.50	90	$0.90	120
1999	$2.75	105	$1.00	130

7. What is the value of the basket in the base year?
   a. $300
   b. $333
   c. $418.75
   d. $459.25
   e. none of the above

8. What are the values of the CPI in 1997, 1998, and 1999, respectively?
    a. 100, 111, 139.6
    b. 100, 109.2, 116
    c. 100, 113.3, 125
    d. 83.5, 94.2, 100
    e. none of the above

9. What is the inflation rate for 1998?
    a. 0%
    b. 9.2%
    c. 11%
    d. 13.3%
    e. none of the above

10. What is the inflation rate for 1999?
    a. 0%
    b. 10.3%
    c. 11%
    d. 13.3%
    e. none of the above

11. The table shows that the 1998 inflation rate is biased upward because of
    a. bias due to the introduction of new goods.
    b. bias due to unmeasured quality change.
    c. substitution bias.
    d. base-year bias.
    e. none of the above.

12. Suppose the base year is changed in the table from 1997 to 1999 (now use the 1999 consumption basket). What is the new value of the CPI in 1998?
    a. 90.6
    b. 100.0
    c. 114.7
    d. 134.3
    e. none of the above

13. Suppose your income rises from $19 000 to $31 000 while the CPI rises from 122 to 169. Your standard of living has likely
    a. fallen.
    b. risen.
    c. stayed the same.
    d. you can't tell without knowing the base year.

14. If the nominal interest rate is 7% and the inflation rate is 3%, then the real interest rate is
    a. -4%.
    b. 3%.
    c. 4%.
    d. 10%.
    e. 21%.

15. Which of the following statements is correct?
    a. The real interest rate is the sum of the nominal interest rate and the inflation rate.
    b. The real interest rate is the nominal interest rate minus the inflation rate.
    c. The nominal interest rate is the inflation rate minus the real interest rate.
    d. The nominal interest rate is the real interest rate minus the inflation rate.
    e. none of the above

16. If inflation is 8% and the real interest rate is 3%, then the nominal interest rate should be
    a. 3/8%.
    b. 5%.
    c. 11%.
    d. 24%.
    e. -5%.

17. Under which of the following conditions would you prefer to be the lender?
    a. The nominal rate of interest is 20% and the inflation rate is 25%.
    b. The nominal rate of interest is 15% and the inflation rate is 14%.
    c. The nominal rate of interest is 12% and the inflation rate is 9%.
    d. The nominal rate of interest is 5% and the inflation rate is 1%.

18. Under which of the following conditions would you prefer to be the borrower?
    a. The nominal rate of interest is 20% and the inflation rate is 25%.
    b. The nominal rate of interest is 15% and the inflation rate is 14%.
    c. The nominal rate of interest is 12% and the inflation rate is 9%.
    d. The nominal rate of interest is 5% and the inflation rate is 1%.

19. If borrowers and lenders agree on a nominal interest rate and inflation turns out to be less than they had expected,
    a. borrowers will gain at the expense of lenders.
    b. lenders will gain at the expense of borrowers.
    c. neither borrowers nor lenders will gain because the nominal interest rate has been fixed by contract.
    d. none of the above.

20. If workers and firms agree on an increase in wages based on their expectations of inflation and inflation turns out to be more than they expected,
   a. firms will gain at the expense of workers.
   b. workers will gain at the expense of firms.
   c. neither workers nor firms will gain because the increase in wages is fixed in the labour agreement.
   d. none of the above.

C. Short-Answer Questions

1. What does the consumer price index attempt to measure? _____

2. What are the steps that one must go through in order to construct a consumer price index? _____
   _____
   _____

3. Which would have a greater impact on the CPI: a 20% increase in the price of Rolex watches or a 20% increase in the price of new cars? Why? _____
   _____

4. Suppose there is an increase in the price of imported Honda automobiles (which are produced in Japan). Would this have a larger impact on the CPI or the GDP deflator? Why? _____
   _____
   _____

5. If Statistics Canada failed to recognize the increase in memory, power, and speed of newer model computers, in which direction would the CPI be biased? What do we call this type of bias? _____
   _____

6. What does the real interest rate measure? _____
   _____

7. Suppose you lend money to your sister at a nominal interest rate of 10% because you both expect the inflation rate to be 6%. Further, suppose that after the loan has been repaid, you discover that the actual inflation rate over the life of the loan was only 2%. Who gained at the other's expense: you or your sister? Why? _____
   _____
   _____
   _____

8. Paying close attention to Question 7, make a general statement with regard to who gains or loses (the borrower or the lender) on a loan contract when inflation turns out to be either higher or lower than expected. _____

_____

_____

9. If workers and firms negotiate a wage increase based on their expectation of inflation, who gains or loses (the workers or the firms) if actual inflation turns out to be higher than expected? Why? _____

_____

_____

D. Practice Problems

1. The following table shows the prices and the quantities consumed in the country known as College Canada. Suppose the base year is 1996. (This is also the year the typical consumption basket was determined.)

Year	Price of books	Quantity of books	Price of pencils	Quantity of pencils	Price of pens	Quantity of pens
1996	$50	10	$1	100	$5	100
1997	$50	12	$1	200	$10	50
1998	$60	12	$1.50	250	$20	20

a. What is the value of the CPI in 1996? _____

b. What is the value of the CPI in 1997? _____

c. What is the value of the CPI in 1998? _____

d. What is the inflation rate in 1997? _____

e. What is the inflation rate in 1998? _____

f. What type of bias do you observe in the CPI and corresponding inflation rates you generated above? Explain. _____

_____

_____

g. If you had a COLA clause in your wage contract based on the CPI calculated above, would your standard of living likely increase, decrease, or stay the same over the years 1996-1998? Why? _____

_____

_____

h. If you personally only consume pens (no paper or pencils), would your standard of living likely increase, decrease, or stay the same over the years 1996-1998? Why? _____

_____

_____

2. The following table contains the CPI (base year 1992) and the average hourly earnings of Canadian workers for the period 1987 through 1997.

Year	CPI	Average Hourly Earnings ($)
1987	81.5	12.75
1988	84.8	13.24
1989	89.0	14.00
1990	93.3	14.72
1991	98.5	15.54
1992	100.0	16.16
1993	101.8	16.45
1994	102.0	16.71
1995	104.2	17.03
1996	105.9	17.37
1997	107.6	17.54

a. Inflate the 1987 average hourly earnings to its equivalent value measured in 1997 prices. _____

_____

_____

b. What happened to real average hourly earnings over this 10-year period?

_____

_____

c. Deflate the 1997 average hourly earnings to its equivalent value measured in 1987 prices. _____

_____

_____

d. Do these two methods give you consistent answers with respect to real average hourly earnings over this 10-year period? _____

_____

_____

3. Suppose that you lend your roommate $100 for one year at 9% nominal interest.

a. How many dollars of interest will your roommate pay you at the end of the year? _____

b. Suppose at the time you both agreed to the terms of the loan, you both expected the inflation rate to be 5% during the year of the loan. What do you both expect the real interest rate to be on the loan? _____

c. Suppose at the end of the year, you are surprised to discover that the actual inflation rate over the year was 8%. What was the actual real interest rate generated by this loan? _____

d. In the case described above, actual inflation turned out to be higher than expected. Which of the two of you had the unexpected gain or loss? Your roommate (the borrower), or you (the lender)? Why? _____
_____
_____

e. What would the real interest rate on the loan have been if the actual inflation rate had turned out to be a whopping 11%? _____
_____

f. Explain what it means to have a negative real interest rate. _____
_____
_____
_____

E. Advanced Critical Thinking

Your father stopped drinking beer in 1995. When you asked him why he stopped, he said, "I stopped because it was just getting too expensive. I started drinking beer in 1975 and beer was only $10.00 per case. The last case I bought in 1995 was $24.00, and I just couldn't justify spending twice as much on beer as I used to."

1. In 1975 the CPI was 34.5. In 1995 the CPI was 104.2. What is wrong with his explanation? _____
_____
_____

2. What is the equivalent cost of a 1975 case of beer measured in 1995 prices? _____
_____
_____

3. What is the equivalent cost of a 1995 case of beer measured in 1975 prices? _____
_____
_____

4. Do both methods give you the same conclusion? _____
_____
_____

5. The preceding example demonstrates what economists refer to as "money illusion." Why do you think economists might choose the phrase "money illusion" to describe this behaviour? _____

_____

_____

III. Solutions

A. True/False Questions

1. T
2. F; military helicopters are not consumer goods.
3. F; the CPI tends to overstate the cost of living because people substitute toward cheaper goods.
4. F; prices in the CPI are weighted according to how much consumers buy of each and food is a larger portion of the consumption basket.
5. T
6. F; the CPI tends to overstate the effects of inflation.
7. F; the industrial product price index measures the price of inputs purchased by businesses.
8. T
9. T
10. F; the largest category is shelter.
11. F; if inflation exceeds the nominal interest rate, the real interest rate is negative.
12. T
13. T
14. F; borrowers will gain at the expense of lenders.
15. T

B. Multiple-Choice Questions

1. d	6. a	11. c	16. c
2. a	7. a	12. a	17. d
3. b	8. c	13. b	18. a
4. c	9. d	14. c	19. b
5. c	10. b	15. b	20. a

C. Short-Answer Questions

1. The overall cost of the goods and services purchased by the typical consumer.

2. Fix the basket, find the prices, compute the basket's cost, choose a base year and compute the index, use the index to calculate the inflation rate.

3. New cars, because they have a greater weight in the typical consumption basket.

4. The CPI, because Hondas are in the typical consumption basket, but Hondas are not included in Canadian GDP.

5. Upward, unmeasured quality change.

6. The interest rate adjusted for the effects of inflation.

7. Expected real interest rate = 4%. Actual real interest rate = 8%. You gained and your sister lost.

8. When inflation is higher than expected, borrowers gain. When inflation is lower than expected, lenders gain.

9. Firms gain, workers lose, because wages didn't rise as much as the cost of living.

D. Practice Problems

1. a. $(\$1100/\$1100) \times 100 = 100$

    b. $(\$1600/\$1100) \times 100 = 145.5$

    c. $(\$2750/\$1100) \times 100 = 250$

    d. $(145.5 - 100)/100 = .455 = 45.5\%$

    e. $(250 - 145.5)/145.5 = .718 = 71.8\%$

    f. Substitution bias, because as the price of pens increased, the quantity consumed declined significantly.

    g. Increase, because this CPI overstates the increase in the cost of living.

    h. Decrease, because the price of pens has increased a greater percentage than the CPI.

2. a. $\$12.75 \times (107.6/81.5) = \$16.83$

    b. They increased slightly because $\$17.54 > \$16.83$

    c. $\$17.54 \times (81.5/107.6) = \$13.29$

    d. Yes, because $\$13.29 > \$12.75$. Real average hourly earnings are higher in 1997.

3. a. $9

    b. $9\% - 5\% = 4\%$

    c. $9\% - 8\% = 1\%$

    d. Your roommate (the borrower) gained, you lost, because the borrower repaid the loan with dollars of surprisingly little value.

    e. $9\% - 11\% = -2\%$

    f. Because of inflation, the interest payment is not large enough to allow the lender to break even (maintain constant purchasing power compared to the day the loan was made).

E. Advanced Critical Thinking

1. He is only looking at the price of beer uncorrected for inflation. The real cost of beer has not risen as much as first appears.

2. $\$10.00 \times (104.2/34.5) = \$30.20$

3. $\$24.00 \times (34.5/104.2) = \$7.95$

4. Yes, each method suggests that, after correcting for inflation, beer was actually more expensive in 1975.

5. When people base decisions on values uncorrected for inflation, there may be an illusion that the cost of living has risen or fallen.

Chapter 7: Production and Growth

I. Chapter Overview

A. Context and Purpose

Chapter 7 is the first chapter in a three-chapter sequence on the production of output in the long run. Chapter 7 addresses the determinants of the growth rate of output, while Chapters 8 and 9 address the market for investment in capital and the market for labour.

The purpose of Chapter 7 is to examine the long-run determinants of both the level and the growth rate of real GDP per person. Along the way, we will discover the factors that determine the productivity of workers and address what governments might do to improve the productivity of their citizens.

B. Helpful Hints

1. *Compound growth is the same as compound interest.* Compound interest is when you earn interest on your previously earned interest. Assuming annual compounding, when you deposit $100 in a bank at 10%, you receive $110 at the end of the year. If you leave it in for two years, you receive compound interest in that you receive $121 at the end of two years — the $100 principal, $10 interest from the first year, $10 interest from the second year, *plus $1 interest on the first year's $10 interest payment.* Next year, interest would be earned not on $100, or $110, but on $121, and so on.

   In like manner, after a number of years, a faster growing economy is applying its percentage growth rate to a much larger base (size of economy) and total output accelerates away from economies that are growing more slowly. For example, applying the rule of 70, an economy that is growing at 1% should double in size after about 70 years (70/1). An economy growing at 4% should double in size every 17½ years (70/4). After 70 years, the 4% growth economy is 16 times its original size while the 1% growth economy is only twice its original size. If both economies started at the same size, the 4% growth economy is now 8 times the size of the 1% growth economy thanks to compound growth.

2. *A simple example more clearly defines the factors of production.* The simpler the production process, the easier it is to separate and analyze the factors of production. For example, suppose output is "holes dug in the ground." Then the production function is:

$$Y = A \, F(L, K, H, N)$$

where Y is the number of holes dug, A is technological knowledge, L is labour, K is physical capital, H is human capital, N is natural resources, and F is a mathematical function that relates how the inputs are combined to produce output. If we have more workers, there is an increase in L, and Y would increase. If we have more shovels, there is an increase in K, and Y would increase. If workers are educated so that more of them dig with the spaded end of the shovel as opposed to digging with the handle, there is an increase in H, and Y would increase (note, the number of workers and the number of shovels is unchanged). If our country has softer soil so that digging is easier here, N is larger and, therefore, Y is larger. Finally, if we discover that it is more productive to dig after it rains rather than during a drought, there is an increase in A, and Y should increase.

II. Self-Testing Challenges

A. True/False Questions

_____1.   The United States should grow faster than Canada because the United States has a larger economy.

_____2.   Growth accumulates over time because of compounding.

_____3.   The "rule of 70" suggests that output doubles every seventy years in the average industrialized country.

_____4.   Human capital refers to human-made capital such as tools and machinery, as opposed to natural capital such as rivers and timber.

_____5.   If a production function exhibits constant returns to scale, then doubling all of the inputs doubles the output.

_____6.   If you deposit $100 at your bank and the account generates 10% annual interest, it will be worth $200 in about seven years.

_____7.   An increase in capital should cause the growth rate of a relatively poor country to increase more than that of a rich country.

_____8.   An increase in the rate of saving and investment permanently increases a country's rate of growth.

_____9.   A country can only increase its level of investment by increasing its saving.

_____10. The only factor of production that is not "produced" is natural resources.

_____11. Investment in human capital and technology may be particularly productive because of spill-over effects, or externalities.

_____12. If Germans invest in the Canadian economy by building a new automotive parts factory, Canadian GDP will rise by more than Canadian GNP.

_____13. Most economists believe that inward-oriented policies that protect infant industries improve the growth rates of developing nations.

_____14. A population that is growing very quickly is a characteristic of a rich nation because only rich nations can afford to accommodate the additional children.

_____15. The opportunity cost of additional growth is that someone must forgo current consumption.

B. Multiple-Choice Questions

1. A reasonable measure of the standard of living in a country is
   a. real GDP per person.
   b. real GDP.
   c. nominal GDP per person.
   d. nominal GDP.
   e. the growth rate of nominal GDP per person.

2. Many East Asian countries are growing very quickly because
   a. they have enormous natural resources.
   b. they are imperialists and have collected wealth from previous victories in war.
   c. they save and invest an unusually high percentage of their GDP.
   d. they have always been wealthy and will continue to be wealthy, which is known as the "snowball effect."

3. When a nation has very little GDP per person,
   a. it is doomed to being relatively poor forever.
   b. it must be a small nation.
   c. it has the potential to grow relatively quickly due to the "catch-up effect."
   d. an increase in capital will likely have little impact on output.
   e. none of the above.

4. Once a country is wealthy,
   a. it is nearly impossible for it to become relatively poorer.
   b. it may be harder for it to grow quickly because of the diminishing returns to capital.
   c. capital becomes more productive due to the "catch-up effect."
   d. it no longer needs any human capital.
   e. none of the above.

5. Using the rule of 70, if your nominal income grows at 10% per year, your nominal income will double in approximately
   a. 7 years.
   b. 10 years.
   c. 70 years.
   d. 700 years.
   e. there is not enough information to answer this question.

6. Using the rule of 70, if your parents place $10 000 in a deposit for you on the day you are born, how much will be in the account when you retire at 70 years old if the deposit earns 3% per year?
   a. $300
   b. $3000
   c. $20 000
   d. $70 000
   e. $80 000

7. If two countries start with the same real GDP/person, and one country grows at 2% while the other grows at 4%,
    a. one country will always have 2% more real GDP/person than the other.
    b. the standard of living in the country growing at 4% will start to accelerate away from the slower growing country due to compound growth.
    c. the standard of living in the two countries will converge due to diminishing returns to capital.
    d. next year the country growing at 4% will be twice as large as the one growing at 2%.

8. The opportunity cost of growth is
    a. a reduction in current investment.
    b. a reduction in current saving.
    c. a reduction in current consumption.
    d. a reduction in taxes.

9. We should expect an increase in productivity within a nation when there is an increase in each of the following except
    a. human capital/worker.
    b. physical capital/worker.
    c. natural resources/worker.
    d. labour.
    e. technological knowledge.

10. Which of the following statements is true?
    a. Countries may have a different level of GDP/person but they all grow at the same rate.
    b. Countries may have a different growth rate but they all have the same level of GDP/person.
    c. Countries all have the same growth rate and level of output because any country can obtain the same factors of production.
    d. Countries have great variance in both the level and growth rate of GDP/person; thus, poor countries can become relatively rich over time.

11. If a production function exhibits constant returns to scale,
    a. doubling all of the inputs has absolutely no impact on output because output is constant.
    b. doubling all of the inputs doubles output.
    c. doubling all of the inputs more than doubles output due to the catch-up effect.
    d. doubling all of the inputs less than doubles output due to diminishing returns.

12. Copper is an example of
    a. human capital.
    b. physical capital.
    c. a renewable natural resource.
    d. a non-renewable natural resource.
    e. technology.

13. Which of the following describes an increase in technological knowledge?
    a. A farmer discovers that it is better to plant in the spring rather than in the fall.
    b. A farmer buys another tractor.
    c. A farmer hires another day labourer.
    d. A farmer sends his child to agricultural college and the child returns to work on the farm.

14. Our standard of living is most closely related to
    a. how hard we work.
    b. our supply of capital, because everything of value is produced by machinery.
    c. our supply of natural resources, because they limit production.
    d. our productivity, because our income is equal to what we produce.

15. Which of the following is an example of foreign portfolio investment?
    a. A Canadian citizen buys stock in Nortel and Nortel uses the proceeds to buy a new plant.
    b. Honda builds a new plant in Ontario.
    c. A U.S. pension fund buys stock in Air Canada, and Air Canada uses the proceeds to buy new airplanes.
    d. Royal Bank builds a new corporate office building.
    e. None of the above.

16. Which of the following government policies is *least* likely to increase growth in Africa?
    a. increased expenditures on public education
    b. increased restrictions on the importing of Japanese automobiles and electronics
    c. elimination of civil war
    d. reduction of restrictions on foreign capital investment
    e. All of the above would increase growth.

17. If Toyota builds a new plant in Ontario,
    a. Canadian GDP will rise more than Canadian GNP.
    b. Canadian GDP will rise less than Canadian GNP.
    c. Canadian GDP and GNP will both fall because some income from this investment will accrue to foreigners.
    d. there has been an increase in foreign portfolio investment in Canada.
    e. none of the above.

18. If real GDP/person in 1990 is $23 300 and real GDP/person in 1991 is $24 025, what is the growth rate of real output per person over this period?
    a. 2.0%
    b. 3.1%
    c. 5.62%
    d. 18.0%
    e. 18.6%

19. Which of the following expenditures to enhance productivity is most likely to emit a positive externality?
    a. TD Bank buys a new computer.
    b. Susan pays her university tuition.
    c. Esso leases a new oil field.
    d. General Motors buys a new drill press.

20. To increase growth, governments should do all of the following except
    a. promote free trade.
    b. encourage saving and investment.
    c. control population growth.
    d. encourage research and development.
    e. nationalize major industry.

C. Short-Answer Questions

1. Economists measure both the level of real GDP per person and the growth rate of real GDP per person. What different concept does each statistic capture? _____
   _____
   _____
   _____

2. Must poor countries stay relatively poor forever and must rich countries stay relatively rich forever? Why? _____
   _____
   _____

3. If your real income grows at 5% a year, how long will it take for your real income to double? _____

4. What factors determine productivity? Which ones are human produced? _____
   _____
   _____
   _____

5. How does human capital differ from physical capital? _____
   _____
   _____
   _____

6. Explain the opportunity cost of investing in capital. Is there any difference in the opportunity cost of investing in human capital versus physical capital? _____
   _____
   _____
   _____

7. Why does an increase in the rate of saving and investment only increase the rate of growth temporarily? _____

_____

8. If foreigners buy newly issued stock in Molson Breweries and Molson Breweries uses the proceeds to expand capacity by building new plants and equipment, which will rise more: GDP or GNP? Why? What do we call this type of investment?

_____

_____

_____

9. Some economists argue for lengthening patent protection while some economists argue for shortening it. Why might patents increase productivity? Why might they decrease productivity? _____

_____

_____

_____

10. List the policies governments might pursue to increase the productivity of their citizens. Which one is, at the very least, fundamentally necessary as a background in which the other policies may operate? Why? _____

_____

_____

_____

D. Practice Problems

1.
Country	Current real GDP/person	Current growth rate
Northcountry	$15 468	1.98%
Southcountry	$13 690	2.03%
Eastcountry	$6343	3.12%
Westcountry	$1098	0.61%

a. Which country is richest? How do you know? _____

_____

b. Which country is advancing most quickly? How do you know? _____

_____

_____

c. Which country would likely see the greatest benefit from an increase in capital investment? Why? _____

_____

_____

d. Referring to (c): Would this country continue to see the same degree of benefits from an increase in capital investment forever? Why? _____

_____

_____

e. Referring to (d): Why might investment in human capital and research and development fail to exhibit the same degree of diminishing returns as investment in physical capital? _____

_____

_____

f. Which country has the potential to grow most quickly? List some reasons why it may not be living up to potential. _____

_____

_____

g. If real GDP per person in Northcountry next year is \$15 918, what is its annual growth rate? _____

_____

_____

2. Use the "rule of 70" to answer the following questions. Suppose the real GDP/person in Fastcountry grows at an annual rate of 2% and the real GDP/person in Slowcountry grows at an annual rate of 1%.

a. How many years does it take for real GDP/person to double in Fastcountry?

_____

b. If real GDP/person in Fastcountry is \$2000 in 1930, how much will it be in the year 2000? _____

c. How many years does it take for real GDP/person to double in Slowcountry?

_____

d. If real GDP/person in Slowcountry is \$2000 in 1930, how much will it be in the year 2000? _____

e. Use the numbers you calculated above to help explain the concept of compound growth. _____

_____

_____

f. If Fastcountry stopped growing in the year 2000, how many years would it take for the standard of living in Slowcountry to catch that of Fastcountry? _____

_____

_____

3. Imagine a kitchen. It contains a cook, the cook's diploma, a recipe book, a stove and utensils, and some venison harvested from the open range.

    a. Link each object in the kitchen to a general category within the factors of production. _____
    _____
    _____

    b. While the different factors of production exhibit different levels of durability, which one is special in that it does not wear out? _____
    _____
    _____
    _____
    _____

E. Advanced Critical Thinking

You are having a discussion with other students in their early 20s. The conversation turns to a supposed lack of growth and opportunity in Canada when compared to some Asian countries such as Hong Kong and Singapore. Your roommate says, "These Asian countries must have cheated somehow. That's the only way they could have possibly grown so quickly."

1. Have you learned anything in this chapter that would make you question your roommate's assertion? _____
    _____
    _____

2. The phenomenal growth rate of Japan since World War II has often been referred to as the "Japanese miracle." Is it a miracle or is it explainable? _____
    _____
    _____
    _____

3. Are the high growth rates found in these Asian countries without cost? _____
    _____
    _____

III. Solutions

A. True/False Questions

1. F; growth depends on the rate of increase in productivity.
2. T
3. F; rule of 70 says that if a variable grows at x percent per year, it will double in 70/x years.

4. F; human capital is the knowledge and skills of workers.
5. T
6. T
7. T
8. F; due to diminishing returns to capital, growth rises temporarily.
9. F; it can attract foreign investment.
10. T
11. T
12. T
13. F; most economists believe that outward-oriented policies improve growth.
14. F; population growth spreads capital more thinly reducing capital per worker and productivity.
15. T

B. Multiple-Choice Questions

1. a	6. e	11. b	16. b
2. c	7. b	12. d	17. a
3. c	8. c	13. a	18. b
4. b	9. d	14. d	19. b
5. a	10. d	15. c	20. e

C. Short-Answer Questions

1. Level of real GDP/person measures standard of living. Growth rate measures rate of advance of the standard of living.

2. No. Since growth rates vary widely across countries, rich can become relatively poorer and poor can become relatively richer.

3. 70/5 = 14 years.

4. Physical capital per worker, human capital per worker, natural resources per worker, and technological knowledge. All except natural resources.

5. Human capital is the knowledge and skills of the worker. Physical capital is the stock of equipment and structures.

6. Someone must forgo current consumption. No, someone must save instead of consume regardless of whether education or machines are purchased with the saving.

7. Because there are diminishing returns to physical capital.

8. GDP. GNP measures only the income of Canadians while GDP measures income generated inside Canada. Therefore, GDP will rise more than GNP because some of the profits from the capital investment will accrue to foreigners in the form of dividends. Foreign portfolio investment.

9. Patents provide a property right to an idea; therefore, people are willing to invest in research and development because it is more profitable. Research and development is a public good once the information is disseminated.

10. Encourage saving and investment, investment from abroad, education, free trade, research and development, protect property rights and establish political stability. Property rights and political stability are necessary for there to be any incentive to save, invest, trade, or educate.

D. Practice Problems

1. a.   Northcountry, because it has the largest real GDP per person.

    b.   Eastcountry, because it has the largest growth rate.

    c.   Westcountry is the poorest and likely has the least capital. Since capital exhibits diminishing returns, it is most productive when it is relatively scarce.

    d.   No. Because of diminishing returns to capital, the additional growth from increasing capital declines as a country has more capital.

    e.   Human capital emits a positive externality. Research and development is a public good after dissemination.

    f.   Westcountry, because it is currently the poorest and could easily benefit from additional capital. It may have trade restrictions (inward-oriented policies), a corrupt or unstable government, few courts, and a lack of established property rights, etc.

    g.   ($15 918 − $15 468)/$15 468 = 0.029 = 2.9%

2. a.   70/2 = 35 years.

    b. $8000.

    c.   70/1 = 70 years.

    d. $4000.

    e.   Fastcountry adds $2000 to its GDP in the first 35 years. Growing at the same percent, it adds $4000 to its GDP over the next 35 years because the same growth rate is now applied to a larger base.

    f.   Another 70 years.

3. a. cook = labour, diploma = human capital, recipes = technological knowledge, stove and utensils = capital, venison = natural resource.

    b. Recipes (technological knowledge) never wear out. Labour and human capital die, the stove and utensils wear out slowly, and the venison is used up (although probably renewable).

E. Advanced Critical Thinking

1. Yes. There are many sources of growth and a country can influence all of them except natural resources.

2. Japan's growth is explainable. Indeed, all of the high growth Asian countries have extremely high investment as a percent of GDP.

3. No. The opportunity cost of investment is that someone must forgo current consumption in order to save and invest.

Chapter 8: Saving, Investment,
and the Financial System

I. Chapter Overview

A. Context and Purpose

Chapter 8 is the second chapter in a three-chapter sequence on the production of output in the long run. In Chapter 7, we found that capital and labour are among the primary determinants of output in the long run. For this reason, Chapter 8 addresses the market for saving and investment in capital, while Chapter 9 will address the market for labour.

The purpose of Chapter 8 is to show how saving and investment are coordinated by the loanable funds market. Within the framework of the loanable funds market, we are able to see the effect of taxes and government budget deficits and surpluses on saving, investment, the accumulation of capital, and ultimately, the growth rate of output.

B. Helpful Hints

1. *A financial intermediary is a middleperson.* An intermediary is someone who gets between two groups and negotiates a solution. For example, we have intermediaries in labour negotiations that sit between a firm and a union. In like manner, a bank is a financial intermediary in that it sits between the ultimate lender (the depositor) and the ultimate borrower (the firm or home builder) and "negotiates" the terms of the loan contracts. Banks don't lend their own money. They lend the depositor's money.

2. *Investment is not the purchase of stocks and bonds.* In casual conversation, people use the word "investment" to mean the purchase of stocks and bonds. For example, "I just invested in ten shares of Royal Bank." (Even an economist might say this.) However, when speaking in economic terms, *investment* is the actual purchase of capital structures and equipment. In this technical framework, when I buy ten shares of newly issued Royal Bank stock, there has been only an exchange of assets — Royal Bank has my money and I have their stock certificates. If Royal Bank takes my money and buys new equipment with it, their purchase of the equipment was economic *investment*.

3. *Don't include consumption loans in the supply of loanable funds.* In casual conversation, people use the word "saving" to refer to their new deposit in a bank. For example, "I just saved $100 this week." (An economist might say this, too.) However, if that deposit were loaned out to a consumer who used the funds to purchase airline tickets for a vacation, there has been no increase in *national saving* (or just *saving*) in a macroeconomic sense. This is because, saving, in a macroeconomic sense, is income (GDP) that remains after *national* consumption expenditures and government purchases ($S = Y - C - G$). No national saving took place if your personal saving was loaned and used for consumption expenditures by another person. Since national saving is the source of the supply of loanable funds, consumption loans do not affect the supply of loanable funds.

4. *Demand for loanable funds is private demand for investment funds.* The demand for loanable funds only includes private (households and firms) demand for funds to invest in capital structures and equipment. When government runs a deficit, it does absorb national saving but it does not buy capital equipment with the funds. Therefore, when government runs a deficit, we consider it a reduction in the supply of loanable funds, not an increase in the demand for loanable funds.

II. Self-Testing Challenges

A. True/False Questions

_____1.   When a business firm sells a bond, it has engaged in equity finance.

_____2.   People who buy stock in a firm have loaned money to the firm.

_____3.   Mutual funds reduce a shareholder's risk by purchasing a diversified portfolio.

_____4.   Federal government bonds pay less interest than corporate bonds because the federal government is a safer credit risk.

_____5.   In a closed economy, saving is what remains after consumption expenditures and government purchases.

_____6.   Public saving is always positive.

_____7.   In a closed economy, investment is always equal to saving regardless of where the saving came from — public or private sources.

_____8.   Investment is the purchase of capital equipment and structures.

_____9.   If you save money this week and lend it to your roommate to buy food for consumption, your act of personal saving has increased national saving.

_____10. The quantity supplied of loanable funds is greater if real interest rates are higher.

_____11. If the real interest rate in the loanable funds market is temporarily held above the equilibrium rate, desired borrowing will exceed desired lending and the real interest rate will fall.

_____12. A reduction in a budget deficit should shift the supply of loanable funds to the right, lower the real interest rate, and increase the quantity demanded of loanable funds.

_____13. Public saving and the government budget surplus are the same thing.

_____14. If the government wanted to increase the rate of growth, it should raise taxes on interest and dividends to shift the supply of loanable funds to the right.

_____15. An increase in a budget deficit that causes a government to increase its borrowing shifts the demand for loanable funds to the right.

B. Multiple-Choice Questions

1. Which of the following is an example of equity finance?
    a. corporate bonds
    b. provincial government bonds
    c. stock
    d. bank loan
    e. All of the above are equity finance.

2. Credit risk refers to a bond's
    a. term to maturity.
    b. probability of default.
    c. tax treatment.
    d. dividend.
    e. price-earnings ratio.

3. A financial intermediary is a middleperson between
    a. labour unions and firms.
    b. husbands and wives.
    c. buyers and sellers.
    d. borrowers and lenders.

4. National saving (or just saving) is equal to
    a. private saving + public saving.
    b. investment + consumption expenditures.
    c. GDP – government purchases.
    d. GDP – consumption expenditures.
    e. none of the above.

5. Which of the following statements is true?
    a. A stock index is a directory used to locate information about selected stocks.
    b. Longer term bonds tend to pay less interest than shorter term bonds.
    c. Federal government bonds tend to pay less interest than corporate bonds.
    d. Mutual funds are riskier than single stock purchases because the performance of so many different firms can affect the return of a mutual fund.

6. If government spending exceeds tax collections,
    a. there is a budget surplus.
    b. there is a budget deficit.
    c. private saving is positive.
    d. public saving is positive.
    e. none of the above.

7. If GDP = $1000, consumption = $600, taxes = $100, and government purchases = $200, how much is saving and investment?
   a. saving = $200, investment = $200
   b. saving = $300, investment = $300
   c. saving = $100, investment = $200
   d. saving = $200, investment = $100
   e. saving = $0, investment = $0

8. If the public consumes $10 billion less and the government purchases $10 billion more (other things unchanging), which of the following statements is true?
   a. There is an increase in saving and the economy should grow more quickly.
   b. There is a decrease in saving and the economy should grow more slowly.
   c. Saving is unchanged.
   d. There is not enough information to determine what will happen to saving.

9. Which of the following financial market securities would likely pay the highest interest rate?
   a. a government bond issued by the province of Ontario
   b. a mutual fund with a portfolio of blue chip corporate bonds
   c. a bond issued by a blue chip company
   d. a bond issued by a start-up company

10. Investment is
    a. the purchase of stocks and bonds.
    b. the purchase of capital equipment and structures.
    c. when we place our saving in the bank.
    d. the purchase of goods and services.

11. If Canadians become more thrifty, we would expect
    a. the supply of loanable funds to shift to the right and the real interest rate to rise.
    b. the supply of loanable funds to shift to the right and the real interest rate to fall.
    c. the demand for loanable funds to shift to the right and the real interest rate to rise.
    d. the demand for loanable funds to shift to the right and the real interest rate to fall.

12. Which of the following sets of government policies is the most growth oriented?
    a. lower taxes on the returns to saving, provide investment tax credits, and lower the deficit
    b. lower taxes on the returns to saving, provide investment tax credits, and increase the deficit
    c. increase taxes on the returns to saving, provide investment tax credits, and lower the deficit
    d. increase taxes on the returns to saving, provide investment tax credits, and increase the deficit

13. An increase in a budget deficit that causes a government to increase its borrowing
   a. shifts the demand for loanable funds to the right.
   b. shifts the demand for loanable funds to the left.
   c. shifts the supply of loanable funds to the left.
   d. shifts the supply of loanable funds to the right.

14. An increase in a budget deficit will
   a. raise the real interest rate and decrease the quantity of loanable funds demanded for investment.
   b. raise the real interest rate and increase the quantity of loanable funds demanded for investment.
   c. lower the real interest rate and increase the quantity of loanable funds demanded for investment.
   d. lower the real interest rate and decrease the quantity of loanable funds demanded for investment.

15. If the supply of loanable funds is very inelastic (steep), which policy would likely increase saving and investment the most?
   a. an investment tax credit
   b. a reduction in a budget deficit
   c. an increase in a budget deficit
   d. none of the above

16. An increase in a budget deficit is
   a. a decrease in public saving.
   b. an increase in public saving.
   c. a decrease in private saving.
   d. an increase in private saving.
   e. none of the above.

17. If an increase in a budget deficit reduces national saving and investment, we have witnessed a demonstration of
   a. indirect finance.
   b. direct finance.
   c. virtuous circle.
   d. crowding out.

18. If Canadians become less concerned with the future and save less at each real interest rate,
   a. real interest rates fall and investment falls.
   b. real interest rates fall and investment rises.
   c. real interest rates rise and investment falls.
   d. real interest rates rise and investment rises.

19. If a government budget surplus results in faster economic growth and, in turn, higher budget surpluses, we call this
    a. a rising real interest rate.
    b. virtuous circle.
    c. vicious circle.
    d. an indeterminate impact on the real interest rate.

20. If a government budget surplus results in faster economic growth and, in turn, higher budget surpluses, we call this
    a. crowding out.
    b. virtuous circle.
    c. vicious circle.
    d. debt finance.

C. Short-Answer Questions

1. Explain why a mutual fund is likely to be less risky than an individual stock.

   _____

   _____

   _____

2. Which is likely to give you a greater rate of return: a chequing deposit at a bank or the purchase of a corporate bond? Why? _____

   _____

   _____

   _____

   _____

3. What is the difference between debt finance and equity finance? Provide an example of each. _____

   _____

   _____

4. What is meant by the words "saving" and "investment" in the national income accounts and how does it differ from the casual use of the words? _____

   _____

   _____

   _____

   _____

5. In a closed economy, why can't investment ever exceed saving? _____

   _____

   _____

   _____

6. What is private saving? What is public saving? _____
   _____
   _____

7. Utilizing the national income identities, if government purchases were to rise, and if output, taxes, and consumption were to remain unchanged, what would happen to national saving, investment, and growth? _____
   _____
   _____

8. Suppose Canadians become more frugal. That is, they consume a smaller percent of their income and save a larger percent. Describe the changes in the loanable funds market. What would likely happen to growth? _____
   _____
   _____
   _____

9. Suppose government runs a larger budget surplus. Describe the changes in the loanable funds market. What would likely happen to growth? _____
   _____
   _____
   _____

10. An increase in a government's budget deficit forces a government to borrow more. Why doesn't an increase in a deficit increase the demand for loanable funds in the loanable funds market? _____
    _____
    _____
    _____

11. What is the fundamental difference between financial markets and financial intermediaries? _____
    _____
    _____

D. Practice Problems

1. Fly-by-night Corporation is in need of capital funds to expand its production capacity. It is selling short- and long-term bonds and is issuing stock. You are considering the prospect of helping finance their expansion.

   a. If you are buying both short- and long-term to maturity bonds from Fly-by-night, from which bond would you demand a higher rate of return: short- or long-term? Why? _____
      _____
      _____

b. If the Canadian Bond Rating Service lowered the credit worthiness of Fly-by-night, would this affect the rate of return you would demand when buying their bonds? Why? _____

_____

_____

_____

c. If Fly-by-night is issuing both stocks and bonds, from which would you expect to earn the higher rate of return over the long run? Why? _____

_____

_____

_____

d. Which would be safer: Putting all of your personal saving into Fly-by-night stock, or putting all of your personal saving into a mutual fund that has some Fly-by-night stock in its portfolio? Why? _____

_____

_____

2. Use the saving and investment identities from the National Income Accounts to answer the following questions. Suppose the following values are from the national income accounts of a country with a closed economy. (All values are in billions.)

Y = $600
T = $100
C = $400
G = $120

a. What is the value of saving and investment in this country? _____

_____

_____

b. What is the value of private saving? _____

_____

_____

c. What is the value of public saving? _____

_____

_____

d. Is government budget policy contributing to growth in this country or harming it? Why? _____

_____

e. Why don't countries reduce their budget deficits? _____

_____

3. The following information describes a loanable funds market. (Values are in billions.)

Real interest rate	Quantity of loanable funds supplied	Quantity of loanable funds demanded
6%	$130	$ 70
5%	$120	$ 80
4%	$100	$100
3%	$ 80	$120
2%	$ 60	$150

a. Plot the supply and demand for loanable funds. What is the equilibrium real interest rate and the equilibrium level of saving and investment? _____

_____

_____

_____

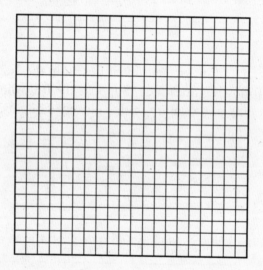

b. What "market forces" will not allow 2% to be the real interest rate? _____

_____

_____

_____

c. Suppose government suddenly increases its budget deficit by $40 billion. What is the new equilibrium real interest rate and equilibrium level of saving and investment? (Show graphically.) _____

_____

_____

_____

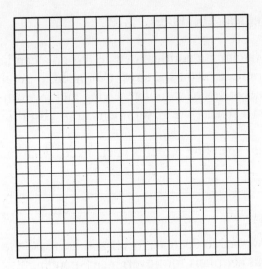

d. Starting at the original equilibrium, suppose the government enacts an investment tax credit that stimulates the demand for loanable funds for capital investment by $40 billion at any real interest rate. What is the new equilibrium real interest rate and equilibrium level of saving and investment? (Show graphically.) _____

_____

_____

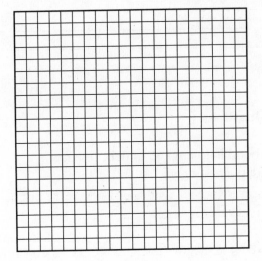

e. With regard to (c) and (d), which policy is most likely to increase growth? Why? _____

_____

_____

_____

E. Advanced Critical Thinking

You are watching a political debate. When a candidate is questioned about her position on economic growth, she says, "We need to get this country growing again. We need to use tax incentives to stimulate saving and investment, and we need to get that budget deficit down so that the government stops absorbing our nation's saving."

1. If government spending remains unchanged, what inconsistency is implied by her statement? _____

_____

_____

2. If she truly wishes to decrease taxes and decrease the budget deficit, what has she implied about her plans for government spending? _____

_____

_____

3. If policymakers want to increase growth, and if policymakers have to choose between tax incentives to stimulate saving and tax incentives to stimulate investment, what might they want to know about supply and demand in the loanable funds market before making their decision? Explain. _____

_____

_____

_____

_____

_____

III. Solutions

A. True/False Questions

1. F; to sell a bond is to engage in debt finance.
2. F; stockholders are owners.
3. T
4. T
5. T
6. F; public saving is negative when there is a government budget deficit.
7. T
8. T
9. F; consumption loans do not increase national saving.
10. T
11. F; desired lending exceeds desired borrowing.
12. T
13. T
14. F; it should lower taxes on interest and dividends.
15. F; it decreases the supply of loanable funds.

B. Multiple-Choice Questions

1. c	6. b	11. b	16. a
2. b	7. a	12. a	17. d
3. d	8. c	13. c	18. c
4. a	9. d	14. a	19. d
5. c	10. b	15. b	20. b

C. Short-Answer Questions

1. Because a mutual fund is diversified. When one stock in the fund is performing poorly, it is likely that another stock is performing well.

2. A corporate bond, because the bond is riskier and because "direct" lending through a financial market has fewer overhead costs than "indirect" lending through an intermediary.

3. Debt finance is borrowing, such as, when a firm sells a bond. Equity finance is taking on additional partners, such as, when a firm sells stock.

4. Saving is what remains after consumption and government purchases. Investment is the purchase of equipment and structures. In casual conversation, saving is what remains out of our income (even if someone else borrows it for consumption) and investment is the purchase of stocks and bonds.

5. Because saving is the GDP left over after consumption expenditures and government purchases, and this is the limit of the output available to be used to purchase equipment and structures.

6. Private saving $= Y - T - C$, public saving $= T - G$.

7. Public saving would decrease and cause national saving and investment to decrease by the same amount, slowing growth.

8. The supply of loanable funds would shift right, the real interest rate would fall, and the quantity demanded of loanable funds to purchase capital would increase. Growth would increase.

9. The supply of loanable funds would shift right, the real interest rate would fall, and the quantity demanded of loanable funds to purchase capital would increase. Growth would increase.

10. The demand for loanable funds is defined as *private* demand for borrowing to purchase capital equipment and structures. An increase in a deficit absorbs saving and reduces the supply of loanable funds.

11. In a financial market, savers lend directly to borrowers. Through financial intermediaries, savers lend to an intermediary who then lends to the ultimate borrower.

D. Practice Problems

1. a. Long-term, because it is more likely that you may need to sell the long-term bond before maturity at a depressed price.

   b. Yes, the credit risk has increased and lenders would demand a higher rate of return.

   c. Owners of stock demand a higher rate of return because it is riskier.

   d. It is safer to put money in a mutual fund because it is diversified (not all of your eggs in one basket).

2. a. ($600 – $100 – $400) + ($100 – $120) = $80 billion

   b. $600 – $100 – $400 = $100 billion

   c. $100 – $120 = –$20 billion

   d. It is harming growth because public saving is negative so less is available for investment.

   e. Because politicians can't agree whether to increase taxes or decrease spending.

3. a. Equilibrium real interest rate = 4%, equilibrium S and I = $100 billion.

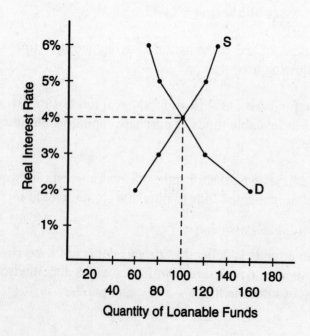

b. At 2% interest, the quantity demanded of loanable funds exceeds the quantity
    supplied by $90 billion. This excess demand for loans (borrowing) will drive
    interest rates up to 4%.

c. Equilibrium real interest rate = 5%, equilibrium S and I = $80 billion.

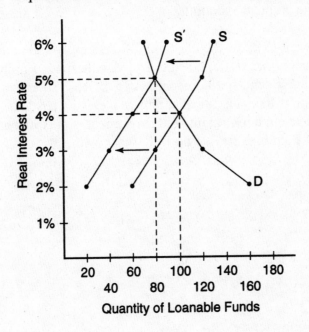

d. Equilibrium real interest rate = 5%, equilibrium S and I = $120 billion.

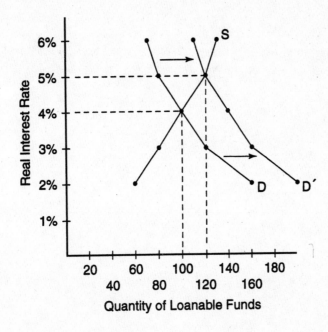

e. An investment tax credit, because it shifts the demand for loanable funds to
    invest in capital to the right, raising the level of investment in capital and
    stimulating growth.

E. Advanced Critical Thinking

1. Tax incentives to stimulate saving and investment require a reduction in taxes. This would increase the deficit, which would reduce national saving and investment.

2. She plans to reduce government spending.

3. Policymakers would want to know the elasticity of the supply and demand curves. If loanable funds demand is inelastic, changes in loanable funds supply have little effect on saving and investment, so tax incentives to increase saving at each interest rate do little for growth. If loanable funds supply is inelastic, changes in loanable funds demand have little effect on saving and investment, so tax incentives to increase investment at each interest rate do little for growth.

Chapter 9: Unemployment and Its Natural Rate

I. Chapter Overview

A. Context and Purpose

Chapter 9 is the third chapter in a three-chapter sequence on the level and growth of output in the long run. In Chapter 7, we learned that capital and labour are among the primary determinants of output and growth. In Chapter 8, we addressed how saving and investment in capital goods affect the production of output. In Chapter 9, we see how full utilization of our labour resources improves the level of production and our standard of living.

The purpose of Chapter 9 is to introduce you to the labour market. We will see how economists measure the performance of the labour market with unemployment statistics. We will also examine the four factors that cause unemployment in the long run, and the effects of government policies on the natural rate of unemployment.

B. Helpful Hints

1. *Moral hazard and adverse selection are best illustrated by insurance.* Suppose companies that sell dental insurance charge the same rate to everyone. Who would buy dental insurance? If everyone is charged the same rate, dental insurance would be a good value for people with serious forms of dental disease, and a poor value for people with healthy teeth and gums. Thus, unhealthy people would tend to buy insurance and healthy people would not. Equal insurance premiums create *adverse selection* because only those with poor teeth or gum disease buy insurance. In the labour market, a firm that pays a low wage creates adverse selection because less productive workers apply for those jobs.

    Furthermore, does someone with dental insurance have an incentive to brush and floss his or her teeth after every meal? No, the insurance creates a *moral hazard* because it gives someone an incentive to undertake less than desirable effort in the daily care of his or her teeth, since the insurance company will bear the financial cost if various types of dental problems arise. In the labour market, a firm that pays a low wage creates a moral hazard because the low wage creates an incentive for workers to undertake an undesirable effort in their job performance.

2. *Job search takes time even at the competitive equilibrium wage.* Minimum-wage laws, unions, and efficiency wages all create an excess supply of labour, called structural unemployment, by holding the wage above the competitive equilibrium wage. However, the frictional unemployment that arises from the process of job search occurs at the competitive equilibrium wage because it is inevitable that it takes time for workers and firms to match regardless of the wage.

3. *The natural rate of unemployment is persistent, not constant.* Minimum-wage laws, unions, efficiency wages, and job search all have an impact on the natural rate of unemployment. Therefore, the natural rate will change as government policies, institutions, and behaviours change. But since policies, institutions, and behaviours change slowly, so does the natural rate of unemployment. Note then, that the natural rate is estimated to have been as low as 4% in the late 1960s, and as high as 8% in the late 1980s.

II. Self-Testing Challenges

A. True/False Questions

_____1. The natural rate of unemployment is the amount of unemployment that won't go away on its own, even in the long run.

_____2. If the unemployment rate falls, we can be certain that more workers have jobs.

_____3. In post-World War II Canada, the labour-force participation rate has been rising for women and has been falling for men.

_____4. The unemployment rate is about the same for the Atlantic region and the Western region of Canada.

_____5. A minimum wage is likely to have a greater impact on the market for skilled workers than on the market for unskilled workers.

_____6. The presence of a union tends to raise the wage for insiders and lower the wage for outsiders.

_____7. A union is a labour cartel.

_____8. Unions may increase efficiency in some circumstances because they decrease the cost of bargaining between labour and management.

_____9. An efficiency wage is like a minimum wage in that firms are required by legislation to pay it.

_____10. Paying efficiency wages tends to increase worker turnover because workers can get continually higher wages if they "job hop."

_____11. If a firm pays the low competitive equilibrium wage, their worker pool may suffer from adverse selection because poor quality candidates tend to apply for their job openings.

_____12. If wages were always at the competitive equilibrium, there would be absolutely no unemployment.

_____13. If there are "discouraged workers," the measured unemployment rate overstates true unemployment.

_____14. The presence of Employment Insurance tends to decrease the unemployment rate because recipients of insurance benefits are not counted in the labour force.

_____15. Whenever the wage rises above the competitive equilibrium, regardless of the source, the result is structural unemployment.

B. Multiple-Choice Questions

1. The amount of unemployment that the economy normally experiences is known as
   a. efficiency wage unemployment.
   b. union unemployment.
   c. cyclical unemployment.
   d. the natural rate of unemployment.

2. According to Statistics Canada, a husband who chooses to stay home and take care of the household is
   a. unemployed.
   b. employed.
   c. not in the labour force.
   d. a discouraged worker.

Use the following table for questions 3 through 5. Numbers are in millions.

Total population	29.7
Adult population	21.2
Number of unemployed	1.2
Number of employed	12.1

3. The labour force is
   a. 12.1 million.
   b. 13.3 million.
   c. 20.0 million.
   d. 21.2 million.
   e. none of the above.

4. The unemployment rate is
   a. 5.7%.
   b. 6.0%.
   c. 9.0%.
   d. 9.9%.
   e. not enough information to answer

5. The labour-force participation rate is
   a. 40.7%.
   b. 44.8%.
   c. 57.1%.
   d. 62.7%.
   e. none of the above.

6. An accountant with a CA designation that has been unable to find work for so long that she has stopped looking for work is considered to be
   a. employed.
   b. unemployed.
   c. not in the labour force.
   d. not in the adult population.

7. Which of the following statements is true?
   a. Women tend to have a lower labour force participation rate than men.
   b. The labour force participation rate of men is rising.
   c. Most spells of unemployment are long-term but most unemployment observed at any given time is short-term.
   d. All of the above are true.

8. A minimum-wage law tends to
   a. create more unemployment in high-skill job markets than in low-skill job markets.
   b. create more unemployment in low-skill job markets than in high-skill job markets.
   c. have no impact on unemployment as long as it is set above the competitive equilibrium wage.
   d. help all teenagers because they receive a higher wage than they would otherwise.

9. Which of the following sources of unemployment is *not* based on the wage being held above the competitive equilibrium wage?
   a. unemployment due to job search
   b. unemployment due to minimum-wage laws
   c. unemployment due to unions
   d. unemployment due to efficiency wages

10. If, for any reason, the wage is held above the competitive equilibrium wage,
    a. unions will likely strike and the wage will fall to equilibrium.
    b. the quality of workers will fall due to the adverse selection of workers in the applicant pool.
    c. the quantity of labour supplied will exceed the quantity of labour demanded and there will be structural unemployment.
    d. the quantity of labour demanded will exceed the quantity of labour supplied and there will be a labour shortage.

11. A "reservation wage" is the
    a. maximum wage the firm is willing to pay.
    b. minimum wage the worker is willing to accept.
    c. tip necessary to get a waiter to reserve a table.
    d. competitive equilibrium wage.

12. Which of the following government policies would *fail* to lower the unemployment rate?
    a. reduce unemployment benefits
    b. establish employment agencies
    c. establish worker training programs
    d. raise the minimum wage

13. Sectoral shifts tend to raise which type of unemployment?
    a. frictional unemployment
    b. structural unemployment
    c. cyclical unemployment
    d. Sectoral shifts do not increase unemployment.

14. Which of the following is an example of "moral hazard"?
    a. At a low wage, a worker quits to find a better job.
    b. At a low wage, a worker sleeps when the boss is not looking because the worker is not deeply concerned about being fired.
    c. At a low wage, only poorly qualified workers ever apply for this job.
    d. At a low wage, a worker cannot afford a healthy diet so the worker falls asleep at work due to a lack of energy.

15. Which of the following is an example of "adverse selection?"
    a. At a low wage, a worker quits to find a better job.
    b. At a low wage, a worker sleeps when the boss is not looking because the worker is not deeply concerned about being fired.
    c. At a low wage, only poorly qualified workers ever apply for this job.
    d. At a low wage, a worker cannot afford a healthy diet so the worker falls asleep at work due to a lack of energy.

16. Unions might increase efficiency in the case where they
    a. raise the wage for insiders above the competitive equilibrium.
    b. offset the market power of a large firm in a company town.
    c. lower the wage of local outsiders.
    d. threaten a strike but don't actually follow through so there are no lost hours of work.

17. Which of the following statements about efficiency wage theory is true?
    a. Firms do not have a choice about whether they pay efficiency wages or not because these wages are determined by law.
    b. Paying the lowest possible wage is always the most efficient (profitable).
    c. Paying above the competitive equilibrium wage creates a moral hazard because it causes workers to shirk their responsibilities.
    d. Paying above the competitive equilibrium wage may improve worker health, lower worker turnover, improve worker quality, and increase worker effort.

18. Unions tend to increase the disparity in pay between insiders and outsiders by
    a. increasing the wage in the unionized sector, which may create an increase in the supply of workers in the non-unionized sector.
    b. increasing the wage in the unionized sector, which may create a decrease in the supply of workers in the non-unionized sector.
    c. decreasing the demand for workers in the unionized sector.
    d. increasing the demand for workers in the unionized sector.

19. Which of the following types of unemployment will exist even if the wage is at the competitive equilibrium?
    a. unemployment due to minimum-wage laws
    b. unemployment due to unions
    c. unemployment due to efficiency wages
    d. unemployment due to job search

20. If Employment Insurance were so generous that it paid laid-off workers 95% of their regular salary,
    a. measured unemployment would probably understate true unemployment.
    b. measured unemployment would probably overstate true unemployment.
    c. there would be no impact on measured unemployment.
    d. frictional unemployment would fall.
    e. none of the above.

C. Short-Answer Questions

1. Name two reasons why the unemployment rate is an imperfect measure of joblessness. _____
_____
_____
_____

2. Explain the statement, "Most spells of unemployment are short, and most unemployment observed at any given time is long-term." _____
_____
_____
_____

3. Where would a labour union be more likely to increase efficiency rather than reduce it: a small remote town with one large employer or a major city with many employers? Why? _____

_____

_____

4. Name two ways that a union increases the disparity in wages between members and non-members. _____

_____

_____

5. If a company pays a low starting wage for new workers and fewer quality candidates apply, we have seen a demonstration of _____

_____

6. If a company pays a low wage and workers shirk their responsibilities and fail to put forth a desirable level of effort, we have seen a demonstration of _____

_____

7. Does the minimum wage cause much unemployment in the market for accountants? Why? _____

_____

_____

8. Which type of unemployment will occur even if the wage is at the competitive equilibrium? Why? _____

_____

_____

_____

9. How does Employment Insurance increase frictional unemployment? _____

_____

_____

_____

10. How might the government help reduce frictional unemployment? _____

_____

_____

_____

11. Which of the following individuals is most likely to be unemployed for the long term: a buggy-whip maker who loses his job when automobiles become popular, or a waitress who is laid off when a new cafe opens in town? Why? _____

_____

_____

D. Practice Problems

1. Use the following information about Employment Country to answer Question 1. Numbers are in millions.

	1998	1999
Population	223.6	226.5
Adult population	168.2	169.5
Number of unemployed	7.4	8.1
Number of employed	105.2	104.2

   a. What is the labour force in 1998 and 1999? _____
   _____
   _____

   b. What is the labour force participation rate in 1998 and 1999? _____
   _____
   _____

   c. What is the unemployment rate in 1998 and 1999? _____
   _____
   _____

   d. From 1998 to 1999, the adult population went up while the labour force went down. Provide a number of explanations why this might have occurred.
   _____
   _____
   _____
   _____

   e. If the natural rate of unemployment in Employment Country is 6.6%, how much is cyclical unemployment in 1998 and 1999? Is Employment Country likely to be experiencing a recession in either of these years?_____
   _____
   _____
   _____
   _____

2. Suppose the labour market is segmented into two distinct markets: the market for low-skill workers and the market for high-skill workers. Further, suppose the competitive equilibrium wage in the low-skill market is $5.00/hour while the competitive equilibrium wage in the high-skill market is $15.00/hour.

a. If the minimum wage is set at $8.00/hour, which market will exhibit the greatest amount of unemployment? Demonstrate it graphically. _____

_____

_____

b. Does the minimum wage have any impact on the high-skill market? Why?

_____

_____

c. Do your results seem consistent with labour market statistics? Explain. _____

_____

_____

d. Suppose the high-skill market becomes unionized and the new negotiated wage is $18.00/hour. Will this have any affect on the low-skill market? Explain.

_____

_____

_____

_____

_____

3. Answer the following questions about the composition of unemployment.

a. What are some of the sources of unemployment? _____

_____

b. Which type of unemployment is initiated by the firm? _____

_____

c. Why might a firm pay wages in excess of the competitive equilibrium? _____

_____

_____

d. Which type of efficiency wage is unlikely to be relevant to Canada? Why?_____
_____

e. How does job search unemployment differ from the other sources of unemployment?_____
_____

E. Advanced Critical Thinking

You are watching the national news with your roommate. The news anchor says, "Unemployment statistics released by Statistics Canada today show an increase in unemployment from 8.4% to 8.6%. This is the third month in a row where the unemployment rate has increased." Your roommate says, "Every month there are fewer and fewer people with jobs. I don't know how much longer Canada can continue like this."

1. Can your roommate's statement be deduced from the unemployment rate statistic? Why?_____
_____
_____
_____
_____

2. What information would you need to determine whether there are really fewer people with jobs?_____
_____
_____

III. Solutions

A. True/False Questions

1. T
2. F; the unemployment rate falls when unemployed workers leave the labour force.
3. T
4. F; unemployment differs across geographic regions in Canada.
5. F; a minimum wage has a greater impact on low-wage workers.
6. T
7. T
8. T
9. F; efficiency wages are paid voluntarily by firms.
10. F; efficiency wages reduce turnover.
11. T
12. F; there would still be frictional unemployment due to job search.
13. F; the measured unemployment rate understates true unemployment.
14. F; Employment Insurance increases the unemployment rate because it increases frictional unemployment.
15. T

B. Multiple-Choice Questions

1. d	6. c	11. b	16. b
2. c	7. a	12. d	17. d
3. b	8. b	13. a	18. a
4. c	9. a	14. b	19. d
5. d	10. c	15. c	20. b

C. Short-Answer Questions

1. Some people claim to be looking for work just to collect unemployment benefits. Others are discouraged workers and have stopped looking for work due to an unsuccessful search.

2. Many people are unemployed for short periods. A few people are unemployed for very long periods.

3. In a small "company" town where a single company has market power that may depress the wage below the competitive equilibrium. This may need to be offset by organized labour.

4. It raises the wage above the competitive equilibrium in the unionized sector. Some of those unemployed in the unionized sector move to the non-unionized sector increasing the supply of labour and lowering the wage in the non-union sector.

5. Adverse selection.

6. Moral hazard.

7. No, because the competitive equilibrium wage for accountants exceeds the minimum wage and, hence, the minimum wage is not a binding constraint for accountants.

8. Frictional unemployment, because job matching takes time even when the wage is at the competitive equilibrium. Also, continuous sectoral shifts and new entrants into the job market make some job search unemployment inevitable.

9. Unemployed workers might devote less effort to their job search, possibly turn down unattractive job offers, and Employment Insurance benefits influence the decisions of some people to enter the labour force.

10. By establishing government-run employment agencies and worker training programs to retrain workers laid off in the contracting sectors for jobs in growing industries.

11. The buggy-whip maker, because he will have to retrain because the contraction of the buggy-whip business is permanent, while the waitress may just have to relocate, possibly just down the street.

D. Practice Problems

1. a.   1998: 7.4 + 105.2 = 112.6 million
         1999: 8.1 + 104.2 = 112.3 million

    b.   1998: (112.6/168.2) × 100 = 66.9%
         1999: (112.3/169.5) × 100 = 66.3%

    c.   1998: (7.4/112.6) × 100 = 6.6%
         1999: (8.1/112.3) × 100 = 7.2%

    d.   Earlier retirements, students staying in university longer, more parents staying at home with children, discouraged workers discontinuing their job search.

    e.   1998: 6.6% – 6.6% = 0%
         1999: 7.2% – 6.6% = 0.6%

         In 1998, unemployment is "normal" for Employment Country, therefore, there is no recession. However, in 1999, unemployment is above normal (positive cyclical unemployment) so Employment Country may be in a recession.

2. a.   The low-skill market will experience unemployment because there will be an excess supply of labour.

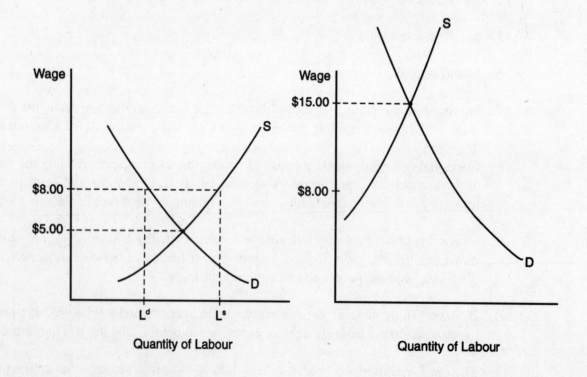

Low-Skill Market   High-Skill Market

b. No, because the competitive equilibrium wage is above the wage floor.

c. Yes. We observe a greater amount of unemployment among low-skill workers who are often young and inexperienced.

d. Yes. The excess supply of skilled workers may cause some skilled workers to move to the unskilled market increasing the supply of labour in the unskilled market, further reducing the competitive equilibrium wage and causing even more unemployment there, at the minimum wage.

3. a. Minimum wage, unions, efficiency wages, job search.

b. Efficiency wages.

c. To improve worker health, lower worker turnover, increase worker effort, improve worker quality.

d. Worker health, because in Canada workers' wages are significantly above subsistence.

e. Job search, or frictional, unemployment exists even when the wage is at a competitive equilibrium.

E. Advanced Critical Thinking

1. No. The unemployment rate is the *ratio* of the number of unemployed to the labour force. If the labour force grows (new graduates, housewives and househusbands entering the labour force) and if only a few of the new members of the labour force find work, then the unemployment *rate* will rise but the number of employed will rise slightly.

2. The number of employed is a component of the labour force and you can get information on that number directly.

Chapter 10: The Monetary System

I. Chapter Overview

A. Context and Purpose

Chapter 10 is the first chapter in a two-chapter sequence dealing with money and prices in the long run. Chapter 10 describes what money is and develops how the Bank of Canada controls the quantity of money. Since changes in the quantity of money influence the rate of inflation in the long run, the following chapter concentrates on the causes and costs of inflation.

The purpose of Chapter 10 is to help you develop an understanding of what money is, what forms money takes, how the banking system helps create money, and how the Bank of Canada controls the quantity of money. An understanding of money is important because changes in the quantity of money affect inflation and interest rates in the long run, and production and employment in the short run.

B. Helpful Hints

1. *Fiat money maintains value due to artificial scarcity.* Gold has value because people desire it for its intrinsic value and because it is naturally scarce (alchemists have never been able to create gold). However, fiat money is cheap and easy to produce. Therefore, fiat money maintains its value only because of self-restraint on the part of the producer. If Canadian dollars are a quality store of value, it is because the paper notes are difficult to counterfeit and the Bank of Canada shows self-restraint in the production of dollars.

2. *Paper notes and coins are considered "currency" only when in the hands of the non-bank public.* When economists use the word currency, we mean "currency in the hands of the non-bank public." When you deposit currency in the bank, you now own a deposit and your paper dollars are now the "reserves" of the bank. Currency in the hands of the non-bank public has decreased while deposits have increased by an equal amount. At this point, the money supply is unaltered because money is the sum of currency (in the hands of the non-bank public) and deposits.

3. *The money multiplier is most easily understood in words.* If we state the relationship between reserves, deposits and the multiplier in words, it clarifies the relationship. Since a fractional reserve system implies that "reserves are some percent of deposits," it follows that "deposits are some multiple of reserves." For example, if reserves are 1/5 (or 20%) of deposits, then deposits are 5 times (or 1/.20) reserves. Since deposit expansion actually takes place due to banks lending some of their reserves, it is most useful to us to think in terms of "deposits are some multiple of reserves."

4. *When dealing with open-market operations, ask yourself, "Who pays?"* It is easiest to remember the impact of open-market operations by asking yourself, "Who pays?" When the Bank of Canada buys a government bond from the public, the Bank of Canada pays with "new dollars" and the money supply expands. When the Bank of Canada sells government bonds, the public pays with dollars and the Bank of Canada "retires" the dollars. That is, the dollars cease to exist when the Bank of Canada receives payment. Note that when the Bank of Canada sells bonds, it is not "issuing" bonds. It is selling existing bonds that were previously issued by the Government of Canada.

II. Self-Testing Challenges

A. True/False Questions

_____1. Money and wealth are the same thing.

_____2. Fiat money is money that is used in Italy.

_____3. Commodity money has value independent of its use as money.

_____4. The M1 money supply is composed of currency and demand deposits.

_____5. When you are willing to go to sleep tonight with $100 in your wallet and you have complete confidence that you can spend it tomorrow and receive the same amount of goods as you would have received had you spent it today, money has demonstrated its function as a medium of exchange.

_____6. Money has three functions: it acts as a medium of exchange, a unit of account, and a hedge against inflation.

_____7. Credit cards are part of the M2 money supply.

_____8. The Bank of Canada is Canada's central bank and is managed by a board of directors, which is appointed by the minister of finance.

_____9. In practice, the Bank of Canada is largely independent of the Canadian government.

_____10. If there is 100% reserve banking, the money supply is unaffected by the proportion of the dollars that the public chooses to hold as currency versus deposits.

_____11. If the Bank of Canada purchases $100 000 of government bonds, and the reserve ratio is 10%, the maximum increase in the money supply is $10 000.

_____12. If the Bank of Canada desires to contract the money supply, it could do one of the following: sell government bonds, or raise the bank rate.

_____13. If the Bank of Canada sells $1000 of government bonds, and the reserve ratio is 10%, deposits could fall by as much as $10 000.

_____14. The Bank of Canada sterilizes foreign exchange purchases by buying government bonds.

_____15. If banks choose to hold extra reserves, lending decreases and the money supply decreases.

B. Multiple-Choice Questions

1. Which of the following is *not* a function of money?
   a. unit of account
   b. store of value
   c. hedge against inflation
   d. medium of exchange

2. The M1 money supply is composed of
   a. currency and demand deposits.
   b. currency, demand deposits, and money market mutual funds.
   c. currency, government bonds, and coins.
   d. currency, savings accounts, and government bonds.
   e. none of the above.

3. An example of fiat money is
   a. gold.
   b. paper dollars.
   c. silver.
   d. cigarettes in a prisoner-of-war camp.

4. Which of the following is not a function of the Bank of Canada?
   a. act as banker to the federal government
   b. act as banker to the commercial banks
   c. issue currency
   d. insure the deposits of the public at Canadian banks
   e. All of these are functions of the Bank of Canada.

5. Commodity money
   a. has no intrinsic value.
   b. has intrinsic value.
   c. is used exclusively in Canada.
   d. is used as reserves to back fiat money.

6. To insulate the governor of the Bank of Canada from short-term political pressure,
   a. the governor is elected by the public.
   b. the governor has life-time tenure.
   c. the governor is supervised by the finance committee of Parliament.
   d. the governor is appointed to a seven-year term.

7. Which of the following statements is true?
   a. The Bank of Canada currently uses the bank rate for long-term control of the money supply.
   b. The Bank of Canada currently uses open-market operations for short-term control of the money supply.
   c. Sterilization is the process of offsetting foreign exchange market operations with open-market operations.
   d. The Bank of Canada has frequently used changes in reserve requirements to control the money supply.
   e. All of the above are true.

8. Required reserves of banks are a fixed percentage of their
   a. loans.
   b. assets.
   c. deposits.
   d. government bonds.

9. If the reserve ratio is 2%, the value of the money multiplier is
   a. 2.
   b. 4.
   c. 10.
   d. 25.
   e. none of the above.

10. Which of the following policy actions by the Bank of Canada would likely increase the money supply?
    a. raising reserve requirements
    b. selling government bonds
    c. decreasing the bank rate
    d. All of these will increase the money supply.

11. Suppose the Bank of Canada buys $200 million American dollars in the foreign exchange market for $270 million Canadian dollars. To sterilize this foreign exchange market operation, the Bank of Canada
    a. lowers the bank rate.
    b. raises the bank rate.
    c. buys government bonds on the open market.
    d. sells government bonds on the open market.
    e. does none of the above.

12. A decrease in the reserve requirement causes
    a. the reserve ratio to rise.
    b. the money supply to fall.
    c. the money multiplier to rise.
    d. reserves to rise.
    e. none of the above.

13. The bank rate is
    a. the interest rate the Bank of Canada pays on the public's deposits.
    b. the interest rate the Bank of Canada charges on loans to banks.
    c. the interest rate banks pay on the public's deposits.
    d. the interest rate the public pays when borrowing from banks.

14. Suppose you write a $1000 cheque on your account to buy a government bond from your friend. If your friend deposits the cheque in her bank, what is the potential change in the money supply if the reserve ratio is 20%?
    a. $1000
    b. $4000
    c. $5000
    d. zero

15. Suppose the Bank of Canada purchases a $1000 government bond from your friend. If your friend deposits the entire $1000 in his bank, what is the potential change in the money supply as a result of the Bank of Canada's action if the reserve ratio is 20%?
    a. $1000
    b. $4000
    c. $5000
    d. zero

16. Suppose all banks maintain a 100% reserve ratio. If an individual deposits $1000 of currency in a bank
    a. the money supply is unaffected.
    b. the money supply increases by more than $1000.
    c. the money supply increases by less than $1000.
    d. the money supply decreases by more than $1000.
    e. the money supply decreases by less than $1000.

17. If the Bank of Canada engages in an open-market purchase and, at the same time, it raises the bank rate,
    a. the money supply should rise.
    b. the money supply should fall.
    c. the money supply should remain unchanged.
    d. we cannot be certain what will happen to the money supply.

18. Given the following T-account, what is the largest new loan this bank can prudently make if the reserve requirement is 10%?

Test Bank

assets		liabilities
reserves	$150	deposits $1000
loans	$850	

a. $0
b. $50
c. $150
d. $1000
e. none of the above

19. The three main tools of monetary policy are
   a. government expenditures, taxation, and reserve requirements.
   b. the money supply, government purchases, and taxation.
   c. coin, currency, and demand deposits.
   d. open-market operations, reserve requirements, and the bank rate.
   e. fiat, commodity, and deposit money.

20. Suppose the Bank of Canada purchases a government bond from someone who deposits the entire amount from the sale in their bank. If the bank holds some of the deposit as excess reserves, the money supply will
   a. rise less than the money multiplier would suggest.
   b. rise more than the money multiplier would suggest.
   c. fall less than the money multiplier would suggest.
   d. fall more than the money multiplier would suggest.

C. Short-Answer Questions

1. What is barter and why does it limit trade? _____

_____

_____

2. What are the three functions of money? _____

_____

3. What are the two basic kinds of money? _____

_____

4. What two main assets are clearly money in Canada and how do they differ from all other assets? (i.e., define money) _____

_____

_____

5. What are the four main jobs of the Bank of Canada? _____

_____

_____

6. What are the three monetary policy tools of the Bank of Canada? _____

_____

_____

7. If the Bank of Canada wished to expand the money supply, how should it adjust each of the three policy instruments described in question 6 above? _____

_____

_____

_____

8. If the Bank of Canada buys $1000 of government bonds from you and you hold all of the payment as currency at home, by how much does the money supply rise?

_____

_____

9. If the Bank of Canada buys $1000 of government bonds from you, you deposit the entire $1000 in a demand deposit at your bank, and banks have a 10% reserve ratio, by how much could the money supply increase?_____

_____

_____

10. Suppose the reserve ratio is 5%. If you write a cheque on your account at Bank 1 to buy a $1000 government bond from your roommate, and your roommate deposits the $1000 in her account at Bank 2, by how much will the money supply change?

_____

_____

11. Suppose there is no deposit insurance. Suppose rumours circulate that banks have made many bad loans and may be unable to repay their depositors. What would you expect depositors and banks to do, and what would their behaviour do to the money supply? _____

_____

_____

D. Practice Problems

1. Suppose the Bank of Canada purchases a Government of Canada Bond from you for $10 000.

   a. What is the name of the Bank of Canada's action? _____

   _____

   _____

   b. Suppose you deposit the $10 000 in First Student Bank. Show this transaction on First Student Bank's T-account.

   First Student Bank

assets	liabilities

c. Suppose the First Student Bank decides to keep 20 percent of its deposits in reserve and to loan out the rest. Show this transaction on the T-account.

First Student Bank

assets	liabilities

d. At this point, how much money has been created from the Bank of Canada's policy action? _____

e. What is the value of the money multiplier? _____

f. After infinite rounds of depositing and lending, how much money could be created from the Bank of Canada's policy action? _____
_____

g. If during the rounds of depositing and lending, some people keep some extra currency and fail to deposit all of their receipts, will there be more or less money created from the Bank of Canada's policy action than you found in part (f)? Why? _____
_____
_____

h. If during the rounds of depositing and lending, some banks choose to hold some of the money as extra reserves, will there be more or less money created from the Bank of Canada's policy action than you found in part (f)? Why? _____
_____
_____

2. Suppose the entire economy contains $1000 worth of five dollar Bank of Canada notes.

a. If people fail to deposit any of the dollars but instead hold all $1000 as currency, how large is the money supply? Explain. _____
_____
_____

b. If people deposit the entire $1000 worth of notes in banks that have a 100% reserve ratio, how large is the money supply? Explain. _____
_____

c. If people deposit the entire $1000 worth of notes in banks that have a 20% reserve ratio, how large could the money supply become? Explain. _____
_____
_____

d. In part (c), what portion of the money supply was created due to the banks? (Hint: $1000 of notes already existed.) _____
_____

e. If people deposit the entire $1000 worth of notes in banks that have a 10% reserve ratio, how large could the money supply become? _____
_____

f. Compare your answer in part (e) to part (c). Explain why they are different.
_____
_____

g. Suppose people deposit the entire $1000 worth of notes in banks that have a 10% reserve ratio. One day, however, the bankers become more cautious about economic conditions and decide to make fewer loans and hold another 10% of deposits as extra reserves. How large could the money supply become?
_____

h. Compare your answer in part (c) to part (g). Are these answers the same? Why? _____
_____
_____

E. Advanced Critical Thinking

Suppose you are a personal friend of David Dodge, current governor of the Bank of Canada. He comes over to your house for lunch and notices your desk. Mr. Dodge is so struck by the beauty of your desk that he simply must have it for his office. Mr. Dodge buys it from you for $1000 and, since it is for his office, pays you with a cheque drawn on the Bank of Canada.

1. Are there more dollars in the economy than before? Why? _____
_____
_____

2. Why do you suppose that the Bank of Canada doesn't buy and sell desks, real estate, and so on, instead of government bonds when they desire to change the money supply? _____
_____
_____
_____

3. If the Bank of Canada doesn't want the money supply to rise when it purchases new furniture, what might it do to offset the purchase? _____
_____
_____

III. Solutions

A. True/False Questions

1. F; money is the spendable portion of one's wealth.
2. F; fiat money is money without intrinsic value.
3. T
4. T
5. F; money demonstrated its function as a store of value.
6. F; store of value, not a hedge against inflation.
7. F; credit cards are not included in the money supply.
8. T
9. T
10. T
11. F; the maximum increase in the money supply is $100\,000 \times (1/0.10) = \$1\,000\,000$.
12. T
13. T
14. F; foreign exchange purchases are sterilized by selling government bonds.
15. T

B. Multiple-Choice Questions

1. c	6. d	11. d	16. a
2. a	7. c	12. c	17. d
3. b	8. c	13. b	18. b
4. d	9. e	14. d	19. d
5. b	10. c	15. c	20. a

C. Short-Answer Questions

1. Barter is trading goods and services directly for other goods and services. It requires a double coincidence of wants.

2. Medium of exchange, unit of account, store of value.

3. Commodity money, fiat money.

4. Currency and demand deposits. They are the assets that are directly spendable or are commonly accepted in trade for goods and services.

5. To issue currency, to act as banker to the commercial banks, to act as banker to the Canadian government, and to control the quantity of money in the economy.

6. Open-market operations, reserve requirements, and the bank rate.

7. Buy Government of Canada bonds, lower the reserve requirement, and lower the bank rate.

8. $1000

9. $1000 \times (1/.10) = $10 000

10. The money supply will not change at all. In this case, reserves are only moved from one bank to another.

11. Depositors will withdraw their deposits reducing bank reserves. Banks will try to hold extra reserves to prepare for the deposit withdrawal. Both will reduce bank lending and the money supply.

D. Practice Problems

1. a. Open-market operations

   b.

   First Student Bank

assets	liabilities
Reserves $10 000	Deposits $10 000

   c.

   First Student Bank

assets		liabilities
Reserves	$2000	Deposits $10 000
Loans	$8000	

   d. $10 000 + $8000 = $18 000

   e. 1/.20 = 5

   f. $10 000 \times 5 = $50 000

   g. Less, because a smaller amount of each loan gets re-deposited to be available to be loaned again.

   h. Less, because a smaller amount of each deposit gets loaned out to be available to be deposited again.

2. a. $1000, because there is $1000 of currency and $0 of deposits.

   b. $1000, because there is now $0 of currency and $1000 of deposits.

   c. $1000 \times (1/.20) = $5000, because $1000 of new reserves can support $5000 worth of deposits.

   d. The potential money supply is $5000, but $1000 was currency already in the system. Thus, an additional $4000 was created by the banks.

e. $1000 \times (1/.10) = \$10\ 000$.

f. Banks can create more money from the same amount of new reserves when the reserve ratio is lower because they can lend a larger portion of each new deposit.

g. $1000 \times 1/(.10 + .10) = \$5000$.

h. Yes, they are the same. With regard to deposit creation, it doesn't matter why banks hold reserves. It only matters how much they hold.

E. Advanced Critical Thinking

1. Yes. When the Bank of Canada purchases anything, they pay with newly created dollars, and there are more dollars in the economy.

2. The transactions costs and storage costs would be staggering. Also, the value of the inventory of "items" would never be certain. The open market for government bonds is much more efficient.

3. The Bank of Canada could sell government bonds of equal value to offset other purchases.

Chapter 11: Money Growth and Inflation

I. Chapter Overview

A. Context and Purpose

Chapter 11 is the second chapter in a two-chapter sequence dealing with money and prices in the long run. Chapter 10 explained what money is and how the Bank of Canada controls the quantity of money. Chapter 11 establishes the relationship between the rate of growth of money and the inflation rate.

The purpose of this chapter is to acquaint you with the causes and costs of inflation. You will find that, in the long run, there is a strong relationship between the growth rate of money and inflation. You will also find that there are numerous costs to the economy from high inflation, but that there is not a consensus on the size of these costs when inflation is moderate.

B. Helpful Hints

1. *The price of money is 1/P.* Since we measure the price of goods and services in terms of money, we measure the price of money in terms of the quantity of goods and services for which money can be exchanged. For example, if a basket of goods and services costs $5, then P = $5. The price of a dollar is then 1/P or 1/5 of the basket of goods. That is, one dollar exchanges for 1/5 of the basket of goods. If the price of the basket of goods doubles so that it now sells for $10, the price of money has fallen to one-half its original value. Numerically, since the price of the basket is now $10, or P = $10, the price of money has fallen to 1/P or 1/10 of the basket of goods. To summarize, when the price of a basket of goods and services double from $5 to $10, the price of money falls by half from 1/5 to 1/10 of the basket of goods.

2. *When dealing with the quantity theory, imagine you are at an auction.* At the end of the auction, we can calculate the number of items sold and the average price of each item sold. Suppose we repeat the auction, only now the doorman doubles the money each buyer takes into the auction — if you had $20, you now have $40, and so on. If all participants spend the same percent of their money as at the prior auction (equivalent to a constant velocity) and if the items available to buy are unchanged (equivalent to a constant real output), what must happen to the average price of goods sold at the auction? Prices at the auction will precisely double, showing that prices are proportional to the quantity of money.

3. *Unexpected inflation works like a tax on future receipts.* We know that unexpected inflation redistributes wealth. Although it can be difficult to remember who wins and who loses on nominal contracts through time, you can always keep things straight if you remember that *unexpected inflation works like a tax on future receipts and a subsidy to future payments.* Therefore, when inflation turns out to be higher than we thought it would be when a loan contract was written, the recipient of the

140

future payments is worse off because he/she receives dollars with less purchasing power he/she had bargained for. The person who borrowed is better off because he/she was able to use the money when it had greater value, yet was allowed to repay the loan with money of lower value. When inflation is higher than expected, wealth is redistributed from lenders to borrowers. When inflation is less than expected, winners and losers are reversed.

This concept can be applied to any contract that extends through time. Consider a labour contract. Recall, when inflation is greater than we expected, those who receive money in the future are harmed and those who pay are helped. Therefore, firms gain at the expense of workers when inflation is greater than anticipated. When inflation is less than expected, winners and losers are reversed.

II. Self-Testing Challenges

A. True/False Questions

_____1. An increase in the price level is the same as a decrease in the value of money.

_____2. The quantity theory of money suggests that an increase in the money supply increases real output proportionately.

_____3. If the price level were to double, the quantity of money demanded would double because people would need twice as much money to cover the same transactions.

_____4. In the long run, an increase in the money supply tends to have an effect on real variables but no effect on nominal variables.

_____5. If the money supply is $500, real output is 2500 units, and the average price of a unit of real output is $2, then the velocity of money is 10.

_____6. The Fisher effect suggests that, in the long run, if the rate of inflation rises from 3% to 7%, the nominal interest rate should increase by 4 percentage points and the real interest rate should remain unchanged.

_____7. An inflation tax is "paid" by those that hold money because inflation reduces the value of their money holdings.

_____8. Monetary neutrality means that a change in the money supply doesn't cause a change in anything at all.

_____9. Inflation erodes the value of people's wages and reduces their standard of living.

_____10. Inflation reduces the relative price of goods whose prices have been temporarily held constant to avoid the costs associated with changing prices.

_____11. The shoeleather costs of inflation should be approximately the same for a medical doctor and for an unemployed worker.

_____12. Inflation tends to stimulate saving because it raises the after-tax real return to saving.

_____13. Countries that spend more money than they can collect from taxing or borrowing tend to print too much money and this causes inflation.

_____14. If inflation turns out to be higher than people expected, wealth is redistributed to lenders from borrowers.

_____15. If the nominal interest rate is 7% and the inflation rate is 5%, the real interest rate is 12%.

B. Multiple-Choice Questions

1. In the long run, inflation is caused by
   a. banks that have market power and refuse to lend money.
   b. governments that raise taxes so high that it increases the cost of doing business and, hence, raises prices.
   c. governments that print too much money.
   d. increases in the price of inputs, such as labour and oil.
   e. none of the above.

2. When prices rise at an extraordinarily high rate, it is called
   a. inflation.
   b. hyperinflation.
   c. deflation.
   d. hypoinflation.
   e. disinflation.

3. If the price level doubles,
   a. the quantity demanded of money falls by half.
   b. the money supply has been cut by half.
   c. nominal income is unaffected.
   d. the value of money has been cut by half.
   e. none of the above.

4. In the long run, the demand for money is most dependent upon
   a. the level of prices.
   b. the availability of credit cards.
   c. the availability of banking outlets.
   d. the interest rate.

5. The quantity theory of money concludes that an increase in the money supply causes
   a. a proportional increase in velocity.
   b. a proportional increase in prices.
   c. a proportional increase in real output.
   d. a proportional decrease in velocity.
   e. a proportional decrease in prices.

6. An example of a real variable is
   a. the nominal interest rate.
   b. the ratio of wages to the price of soda.
   c. the price of corn.
   d. the dollar wage.
   e. all of the above.

7. The quantity equation states that
   a. money × price level = velocity × real output.
   b. money × real output = velocity × price level.
   c. money × velocity = price level × real output.
   d. none of the above.

8. If money is neutral,
   a. an increase in the money supply does nothing.
   b. the money supply cannot be changed because it is tied to a commodity such as gold.
   c. a change in the money supply only affects real variables such as real output.
   d. a change in the money supply only affects nominal variables such as prices and dollar wages.
   e. a change in the money supply reduces velocity proportionately; therefore, there is no effect on either prices or real output.

9. If the money supply grows 5%, and real output grows 2%, prices should rise by
   a. 5%.
   b. less than 5%.
   c. more than 5%.
   d. none of the above.

10. Velocity is
    a. the annual rate of turnover of the money supply.
    b. the annual rate of turnover of output.
    c. the annual rate of turnover of business inventories.
    d. highly unstable.
    e. impossible to measure.

11. Countries that employ an inflation tax do so because
    a. the government doesn't understand the causes and consequences of inflation.
    b. the government has a balanced budget.
    c. government expenditures are high and the government has inadequate tax collections and difficulty borrowing.
    d. an inflation tax is the most equitable of all taxes.
    e. an inflation tax is the most progressive (paid by the rich) of all taxes.

12. An inflation tax
    a. is an explicit tax paid quarterly by businesses based on the amount of increase in the prices of their products.
    b. is a tax on people who hold money.
    c. is a tax on people who hold interest-bearing savings accounts.
    d. is usually employed by governments with balanced budgets.
    e. is none of the above.

13. Suppose the nominal interest rate is 7% while the money supply is growing at a rate of 5% per year. If the government increases the growth rate of the money supply from 5% to 9%, the Fisher effect suggests that, in the long run, the nominal interest rate should become
    a. 4%.
    b. 9%.
    c. 11%.
    d. 12%.
    e. 16%.

14. If the nominal interest rate is 6% and the inflation rate is 3%, the real interest rate is
    a. 3%.
    b. 6%.
    c. 9%.
    d. 18%.
    e. none of the above.

15. If actual inflation turns out to be greater than people had expected, then
    a. wealth was redistributed to lenders from borrowers.
    b. wealth was redistributed to borrowers from lenders.
    c. no redistribution occurred.
    d. the real interest rate is unaffected.

16. Which of the following costs of inflation does not occur when inflation is constant and predictable?
    a. shoeleather costs
    b. menu costs
    c. costs due to inflation-induced tax distortions
    d. arbitrary redistributions of wealth
    e. costs due to confusion and inconvenience

17. Suppose that, because of inflation, a business in Russia must calculate, print, and mail a new price list to its customers each month. This is an example of
    a. shoeleather costs.
    b. menu costs.
    c. costs due to inflation-induced tax distortions.
    d. arbitrary redistributions of wealth.
    e. costs due to confusion and inconvenience.

18. Suppose that, because of inflation, people in Brazil economize on currency and go to the bank each day to withdraw their daily currency needs. This is an example of
    a. shoeleather costs.
    b. menu costs.
    c. costs due to inflation-induced tax distortions.
    d. costs due to inflation-induced relative price variability that misallocates resources.
    e. costs due to confusion and inconvenience.

19. If the real interest rate is 4%, the inflation rate is 6%, and the tax rate is 20%, what is the after-tax real interest rate?
    a. 1%
    b. 2%
    c. 3%
    d. 4%
    e. 5%

20. Which of the following statements is true about a situation where real incomes are rising at 3% per year.
    a. If inflation were 5%, people should receive raises of about 8% per year.
    b. If inflation were 0%, people should receive raises of about 3%.
    c. If money is neutral, an increase in the money supply will not alter the rate of growth of real income.
    d. All of the above are true.
    e. None of the above are true.

C. Short-Answer Questions

1. If the money supply doubles, what must happen in the long run to the quantity of money demanded and the price level? _____
   _____
   _____
   _____

2. Explain the classical dichotomy. _____
   _____
   _____
   _____

3. Within the framework of the classical dichotomy, which type of variables are affected by changes in money and which type are not? What phrase do we use to capture this effect? _____
   _____
   _____
   _____

4. Is money more likely to be neutral in the long run or the short run? Why? _____
    _____
    _____
    _____

5. Suppose the money supply were to increase by 10%. Explain what would happen to
    each variable in the quantity equation. _____
    _____
    _____

6. What are the three sources of revenue a government can use to support its
    expenditures? Which method causes inflation and who bears the burden of this
    method of raising revenue? _____
    _____
    _____

7. In the long run, what does an increase in the growth rate of the money supply do to
    real and nominal interest rates? _____
    _____
    _____

8. Does inflation erode the value of our income and thereby lower our standard of
    living? Explain. _____
    _____

9. What are the costs of inflation when inflation is perfectly anticipated? _____
    _____
    _____
    _____

10. Suppose inflation turns out to be lower than we had expected. Who is likely to gain:
    borrowers or lenders? union workers or firms? Why? _____
    _____
    _____
    _____

11. What is the inconsistency in the following statement? "When inflation is high but
    stable and predictable, inflation does not redistribute wealth." _____
    _____
    _____

12. Does inflation (if correctly anticipated) make borrowers worse off and lenders better
    off when it raises nominal interest rates? Why? _____
    _____
    _____
    _____

D. Practice Problems

1. Use the quantity equation for this problem. Suppose the money supply is $200, real output is 1000 units, and the price per unit of output is $1.

   a. What is the value of velocity?_____

   _____

   b. If velocity is fixed at the value you solved for in part (a), what does the quantity theory of money suggest will happen if the money supply is increased to $400?

   _____

   _____

   _____

   _____

   c. Is your answer in part (b) consistent with the classical dichotomy? Explain.

   _____

   _____

   _____

   _____

   d. Suppose that when the money supply is doubled from $200 to $400, real output grows a small amount (say 2%). Now what will happen to prices? Do prices more than double, less than double, or exactly double? Why?_____

   _____

   _____

   _____

   _____

   e. When inflation gets very high, people don't like to hold money because it is losing value quickly. Therefore, they spend it faster. If when the money supply is doubled, people spend money more quickly, what happens to prices? Do prices more than double, less than double, or exactly double? Why?_____

   _____

   _____

   _____

   _____

   f. Suppose the money supply at the beginning of this problem refers to M1. That is, the M1 money supply is $200. What would the M2 quantity equation look like if the M2 money supply were $500 (and all other values were as stated at the beginning of the problem)? _____

   _____

   _____

   _____

   _____

2. The following questions are related to the Fisher effect.

   a. To demonstrate your understanding of the Fisher effect, complete the following table.

Real interest rate	Nominal interest rate	Inflation rate
3%	10%	
	6%	2%
5%		3%

The following questions about the Fisher effect are unrelated to the table above.

   b. Suppose people expect inflation to be 3% and suppose the desired real interest rate is 4%. What is the nominal rate? _____

_____

   c. Suppose inflation turns out to be 6%. What is the actual real interest rate on loans that were signed based on the expectations in part (b)? _____

_____

_____

   d. Was wealth redistributed to the lender from the borrower or to the borrower from the lender when inflation was expected to be 3% but, in fact, turned out to be 6%? _____

_____

   e. What would have happened had inflation turned out to be only 1%? _____

_____

_____

3. Income taxes treat nominal interest earned on savings as income even though much of the nominal interest is just to compensate for inflation.

   a. To see what this does to the incentive to save, complete the following table for both the low-inflation and high-inflation country.

	Low-inflation country	High-inflation country
Real interest rate	5%	5%
Inflation rate	3%	11%
Nominal interest rate		
Reduced interest due to a 25% tax		
After-tax nominal interest rate		
After-tax real interest rate		

b. In which country is there a greater incentive to save? Why? _____

_____

_____

c. What could the government do to eliminate this problem? _____

_____

_____

E. Advanced Critical Thinking

Suppose you explain the concept of an "inflation tax" to a friend. You correctly tell them, "When a government prints money to cover its expenditures instead of taxing or borrowing, it causes inflation. An inflation tax is simply the erosion of the value of money from this inflation. Therefore, the burden of the tax lands on those who hold money." Your friend responds, "What's so bad about that? Rich people have all the money so an inflation tax seems fair to me. Maybe the government should finance all of its expenditures by printing money."

1. Is it true that rich people hold more money than poor people? _____

_____

_____

2. Do rich people hold a higher percent of their wealth as money than poor people?

_____

_____

_____

3. Does an inflation tax place a greater burden on the poor than on the rich? Why?

_____

_____

4. Are there any other reasons why engaging in an inflation tax is not good policy?

_____

_____

_____

III. Solutions

A. True/False Questions

1. T
2. F; it increases the price level proportionately.
3. T
4. F; the money supply tends to have an effect on nominal variables but not real variables.

5. T
6. T
7. T
8. F; it doesn't cause a change in real variables.
9. F; inflation in incomes goes hand in hand with inflation in prices.
10. T
11. F; the opportunity costs of trips to the bank are greater for a medical doctor.
12. F; inflation tends to reduce the after-tax real return to saving.
13. T
14. F; wealth is redistributed to borrowers from lenders.
15. F; the real interest rate is 2% because 7% − 5% = 2%.

B. Multiple-Choice Questions

1. c	6. b	11. c	16. d
2. b	7. c	12. b	17. b
3. d	8. d	13. c	18. a
4. a	9. b	14. a	19. b
5. b	10. a	15. b	20. d

C. Short-Answer Questions

1. The quantity of money demanded must double to maintain monetary equilibrium. Spending will double on the same amount of goods causing prices to double and the value of money to fall by half.

2. The view that macroeconomic variables can be divided into two groups: real (measured in physical units) and nominal (measured in monetary units).

3. Nominal are affected. Real are not. Monetary neutrality.

4. In the long run, because it takes time for people and markets to adjust prices in response to a change in the money supply. In the short run, mistakes are likely to be made.

5. V remains constant. Y remains constant. M rises by 10% and P rises by 10%.

6. Taxes, borrowing, and printing money. Printing money. Those that hold money because its value decreases.

7. No impact on the real interest rate. Raises the nominal interest rate one-to-one with the increase in the growth rate of money and prices.

8. No. Income is a result of selling labour services, the value of which rises along with other prices during an inflation.

9. Shoeleather costs, menu costs, costs due to relative-price variability that misallocates resources, tax distortions, confusion and inconvenience.

10. Lenders and workers. Those that receive dollars in the future on contract receive dollars of greater value than they bargained for.

11. When inflation is high, it is always unstable and difficult to predict.

12. No. The nominal interest rate adjusts one-to-one with the rise in inflation so that the real rate is unaffected. Neither the borrower nor lender gain.

D. Practice Problems

1. a. $(1000 \times \$1)/\$200 = 5$

    b. $\$400 \times 5 = \$2 \times 1000$, prices will double from $1 to $2

    c. Yes. The classical dichotomy divides economic variables into real and nominal. Money affects nominal variables proportionately and has no impact on real variables. In part (b), prices double, but real output remains constant.

    d. The quantity equation says that nominal output must change in proportion to money. Prices will still rise, but since real output is larger, prices will less than double.

    e. Money has a proportional impact on nominal output if V is constant. If V grows, a doubling of M will cause P to more than double.

    f. $\$500 \times 2 = \$1 \times 1000$, M2 velocity is 2.

2. a.

Real interest rate	Nominal interest rate	Inflation rate
3%	10%	7%
4%	6%	2%
5%	8%	3%

    b. $3\% + 4\% = 7\%$

    c. People would have signed loan contracts for 7% nominal interest. Therefore, $7\% - 6\% = 1\%$.

    d. People expected a real interest rate of 4%, but the actual real interest rate turned out to be 1%. Wealth was redistributed to the borrower from the lender.

    e. The original loan contract would be the same. Thus $7\% - 1\% = 6\%$. The actual real rate is 6% instead of 4% so wealth is redistributed to lenders from borrowers.

3. a.

	Low-inflation country	High-inflation country
Real interest rate	5%	5%
Inflation rate	3%	11%
Nominal interest rate	8%	16%
Reduced interest due to a 25% tax	2%	4%
After-tax nominal interest rate	6%	12%
After-tax real interest rate	3%	1%

    b. In the low-inflation country because the after-tax real interest rate is larger.

    c. They could eliminate inflation or tax only real interest income.

E. Advanced Critical Thinking

1. Yes, rich people probably hold more dollars than poor people.

2. No, by a wide margin, poor hold a larger percent of their wealth as money. In fact, the poor may have no other financial asset at all.

3. An inflation tax places a far greater burden on the poor than on the rich. The rich are able to keep most of their assets in inflation-adjusted interest-bearing assets. We see this in Brazil and Argentina.

4. Inflation imposes many other costs on the economy besides the inflation tax: shoeleather costs, menu costs, tax distortions, confusion, resource misallocation, and wealth redistribution.

Chapter 12: Open-Economy Macroeconomics: Basic Concepts

I. Chapter Overview

A. Context and Purpose

Chapter 12 is the first chapter in a two-chapter sequence dealing with open-economy macroeconomics. Chapter 12 develops the basic concepts and vocabulary associated with macroeconomics in an international setting: net exports, net foreign investment, real and nominal exchange rates, interest rate parity, and purchasing-power parity. The next chapter, Chapter 13, builds an open-economy macroeconomic model that shows how these variables are determined simultaneously.

The purpose of Chapter 12 is to develop the basic concepts macroeconomists use to study open economies. We address why a nation's net exports must equal its net foreign investment. We also address the concepts of the real and nominal exchange rate, develop a theory of exchange rate determination known as purchasing-power parity, and discuss the relationship between Canadian and world interest rates.

B. Helpful Hints

1. *Negative net foreign investment increases domestic investment.* National saving is used to support domestic investment and net foreign investment:

$$S = I + NFI.$$

   If NFI is negative, as it is typically for Canada, it means that foreigners invest more in Canada than Canadians invest abroad. This allows domestic investment to exceed Canada's national saving. For example, suppose saving is $150 billion and net foreign investment is –$20 billion. Domestic investment is $I = \$150 + \$20$ or $170 billion.

2. *Always express nominal and real exchange rates in terms of foreign units relative to domestic units.* Expressing exchange rates in terms of foreign units relative to domestic units helps avoid confusion because a rise in this exchange rate is associated with a rise in the value of the domestic unit. For example, suppose the nominal exchange rate between the lira and the dollar is expressed as 1000 lira/dollar. If the exchange rate rises to 1100 lira/dollar, the value of the dollar has risen.

3. *When generating nominal or real exchange rates, always identify the units of measurement.* A common mistake committed by students when calculating exchange rates (particularly real exchange rates) is to fail to identify the units of measurement throughout the problem and to try to attach the units of measurement at the end of the problem after a numerical solution has been found. This leaves much room for error and confusion. Notice in the real exchange rate example in the textbook about French and Canadian wheat that the units are attached to the numbers throughout. This is not just for your convenience. It is necessary to avoid making mistakes even if you have done it numerous times.

4. *Purchasing-power parity should hold for goods of high value and low transportation costs.* The law of one price applies to goods for which arbitrage is most likely. Hence, we might expect the dollar price of diamonds to be the same in all countries because small deviations in the price of diamonds create substantial profit opportunities. However, large deviations in prices of shoeshines between Vancouver and New York are unlikely to create profit opportunities and a movement of goods or services. While many goods and services are not currently traded across borders, growth in the production and trade of light, high-technology, high-value commodities should increase the applicability of the purchasing-power parity theory.

II. Self-Testing Challenges

A. True/False Questions

_____1.   Net exports are defined as imports minus exports.

_____2.   Canadian net foreign investment falls when Toyota buys stock in Canadian Pacific Hotels.

_____3.   For any country, net exports are always equal to net foreign investment because every international transaction involves an exchange of an equal value of some combination of goods and assets.

_____4.   For a given amount of Canadian national saving, an increase in Canadian net foreign investment decreases Canadian domestic investment.

_____5.   Valuable technologically-advanced goods are less likely to be traded internationally because shipping costs absorb too much of the potential profit.

_____6.   A country that exports more than it imports is said to have a trade deficit.

_____7.   If the yen/dollar exchange rate rises, the dollar has appreciated.

_____8.   If a case of Pepsi costs $8 in Canada and 720 yen in Japan, then according to the purchasing-power parity theory of exchange rates, the yen/dollar exchange rate should be 5760 yen/dollar.

_____9.   If purchasing-power parity holds, the real exchange rate is constant.

_____10.   If Italy's money supply grows faster than Germany's, the value of the lira should rise relative to the value of the mark.

_____11.   If the nominal exchange rate is 2 marks to the dollar, and if the price of a Big Mac is $2 in Canada and 6 marks in Germany, then the real exchange rate is 2/3 German Big Mac per Canadian Big Mac.

_____12.   In order to increase domestic investment, a country must either increase its saving or decrease its net foreign investment.

_____13.   Arbitrage is the process of taking advantage of differences in prices of the same good by buying where the good is cheap and selling where it is expensive.

_____14. Canadian interest rates are slightly higher than U.S. interest rates partly because of higher default risk in Canada.

_____15. If a company based in Canada prefers a strong dollar (a dollar with a high exchange value), it must export more than it imports.

B. Multiple-Choice Questions

1. An economy that interacts with other economies is known as
   a. a balanced trade economy.
   b. an export economy.
   c. an import economy.
   d. a closed economy.
   e. an open economy.

2. Each of the following is a reason why the Canadian economy continues to engage in greater amounts of international trade except which one?
   a. There are larger cargo ships and airplanes.
   b. High-technology goods are more valuable per kilogram and, thus, more likely to be traded.
   c. NAFTA imposes requirements for increased trade between countries in North America.
   d. There have been improvements in technology that have improved telecommunications between countries.
   e. All of the above are reasons for increased trade by Canada.

3. Which of the following statements is true about a country with a trade deficit?
   a. Net foreign investment must be positive.
   b. Net exports are negative.
   c. Net exports are positive.
   d. Exports exceed imports.
   e. None of the above.

4. Which of the following would directly increase Canadian net foreign investment?
   a. Stelco buys a new blast furnace from Japan.
   b. Nortel Networks builds a new distribution facility in Sweden.
   c. Honda builds a new plant in Ontario.
   d. Toyota buys stock in the Bank of Montreal.

5. If Japan exports more than it imports,
   a. Japan's net exports are negative.
   b. Japan's net foreign investment must be negative.
   c. Japan's net foreign investment must be positive.
   d. Japan is running a trade deficit.

6. If Canada saves $100 billion and Canadian net foreign investment is –$20 billion, Canadian domestic investment is
   a. –$20 billion.
   b. $20 billion.
   c. $80 billion.
   d. $100 billion.
   e. $120 billion.

7. If the exchange rate changes from 3 marks per dollar to 4 marks per dollar,
   a. the dollar has depreciated.
   b. the dollar has appreciated.
   c. the dollar could have appreciated or depreciated depending what happened to relative prices in Germany and Canada.
   d. none of the above.

8. Suppose the real exchange rate between Russia and Canada is defined in terms of bottles of Russian vodka per bottle of Canadian vodka. Which of the following will increase the real exchange rate (that is, increase the number of bottles of Russian vodka per bottle of Canadian vodka)?
   a. a decrease in the ruble price of Russian vodka
   b. an increase in the dollar price of Canadian vodka
   c. an increase in the number of rubles for which the dollar can be exchanged
   d. All of the above will increase the real exchange rate.
   e. None of the above will increase the real exchange rate.

9. The most accurate measure of the international value of the dollar is
   a. the yen/dollar exchange rate.
   b. the mark/dollar exchange rate.
   c. the American dollar/Canadian dollar exchange rate.
   d. the franc/dollar exchange rate.
   e. an exchange rate index that accounts for many exchange rates.

10. If the nominal exchange rate between British pounds and Canadian dollars is 0.5 pound per dollar, how many Canadian dollars can you get for a British pound?
    a. 2 dollars
    b. 1.5 dollars
    c. 1 dollar
    d. 0.5 of a dollar
    e. none of the above

11. Suppose the nominal exchange rate between Italian lira and the Canadian dollar is 1000 lira per dollar. Further, suppose that a kilogram of hamburger costs $2 in Canada and 2500 lira in Italy. What is the real exchange rate between Italy and Canada?
    a. 0.5 kg of Italian hamburger/kg of Canadian hamburger
    b. 0.8 kg of Italian hamburger/kg of Canadian hamburger

   c. 1.25 kg of Italian hamburger/kg of Canadian hamburger
   d. 2.5 kg of Italian hamburger/kg of Canadian hamburger
   e. none of the above

12. Which of the following people or firms would be pleased by a depreciation of the Canadian dollar?
   a. a Canadian tourist traveling in Europe
   b. a Canadian importer of Russian vodka
   c. a French exporter of wine to Canada
   d. an Italian importer of Canadian steel

13. Suppose a cup of coffee is 1.5 marks in Germany and $.50 in Canada. If purchasing-power parity holds, what is the nominal exchange rate between marks and dollars?
   a. 1/3 mark per dollar
   b. 3 marks per dollar
   c. 1.5 marks per dollar
   d. 0.75 marks per dollar

14. Which of the following products would likely be the least accurate if used to calculate purchasing-power parity?
   a. gold
   b. automobiles
   c. diamonds
   d. dental services

15. Suppose the money supply in Mexico grows more quickly than the money supply in Canada. We would expect that
   a. the peso should depreciate relative to the dollar.
   b. the peso should appreciate relative to the dollar.
   c. the peso should maintain a constant exchange rate with the dollar because of purchasing-power parity.
   d. none of the above.

16. Suppose a resident of Canada buys a Jaguar automobile from Great Britain and the British exporter uses the receipts to buy stock in Toronto Dominion Bank. Which of the following statements is true from the perspective of Canada?
   a. net exports fall and net foreign investment falls
   b. net exports rise and net foreign investment rises
   c. net exports fall and net foreign investment rises
   d. net exports rise and net foreign investment falls
   e. none of the above

17. Which of the following statements is *not* true about the relationship between national saving, investment, and net foreign investment?
    a. Saving is the sum of investment and net foreign investment.
    b. For a given amount of saving, an increase in net foreign investment must decrease domestic investment.
    c. For a given amount of saving, a decrease in net foreign investment must decrease domestic investment.
    d. An increase in saving associated with an equal increase in net foreign investment leaves domestic investment unchanged.

18. Suppose the inflation rate over the last 20 years has been 9% in Great Britain, 7% in France, and 5% in Canada. If purchasing-power parity holds, which of the following statements is true? Over this period,
    a. the value of the dollar should have fallen compared to the value of the pound and the franc.
    b. the franc should have risen in value compared to the pound and fallen compared to the dollar.
    c. the franc should have fallen in value compared to the pound and risen compared to the dollar.
    d. the value of the pound should have risen compared to the value of the franc and the dollar.
    e. none of the above.

19. If the interest rate in Canada equals the interest rate prevailing in world financial markets, then this is a result of
    a. purchasing-power parity.
    b. net foreign investment.
    c. net exports.
    d. interest-rate parity.
    e. currency appreciation.

20. If the world interest rate is 6% and foreigners believe that there is a higher default risk in Canada, then the interest rate in Canada should be
    a. more than 6%.
    b. 6%.
    c. less than 6%.

C. Short-Answer Questions

1. Identify four reasons why the Canadian economy has engaged in an increasing amount of trade over the last 40 years. _____
    _____
    _____
    _____

2. Define net foreign investment. When foreigners invest in Canada, what happens to the value of Canadian NFI? _____

_____

_____

3. What are the two mutually exclusive locations where national saving can be invested? _____

_____

4. If national saving is held constant, what happens to domestic investment if NFI decreases? Why? _____

_____

5. Suppose the Canadian dollar appreciates relative to world currencies. Would a Canadian importer of fresh produce be pleased or upset? _____

_____

_____

6. In terms of the real exchange rate, what three variables could change to make Canada more competitive internationally? _____

_____

_____

7. Suppose a Chrysler minivan sells for $20 000 Canadian in Canada, and for $16 000 American in the United States. If purchasing-power parity holds, what is the American dollar/Canadian dollar exchange rate? How many Canadian dollars does it take to buy $1.00 American? _____

_____

_____

8. Suppose trade increases between countries. Would this increase or decrease the predictive accuracy of the purchasing-power parity theory of exchange rate determination? _____

_____

_____

9. If the money supply grows at an average annual rate of 5% in Canada and at an average annual rate of 35% in Mexico, what should happen over time to the Mexican peso/dollar exchange rate if purchasing-power parity holds? Why? _____

_____

_____

10. Why might the interest rate in Canada be higher than the interest rate prevailing in world financial markets? _____

_____

_____

D. Practice Problems

1. How would each of the following transactions affect Canadian NFI? Does the transaction affect direct investment or portfolio investment?

   a. Air Canada buys stock in American Airlines. _____
   _____

   b. Bombardier buys steel from a Japanese manufacturer to use in the production of its airplanes. _____
   _____
   _____

   c. Honda expands its plant in Ontario. _____
   _____

   d. A Japanese mutual fund buys shares of stock in Royal Bank. _____
   _____

   e. Nortel Networks builds a plant in Germany. _____
   _____

2. Suppose a resident of Great Britain buys a computer from a Canadian manufacturer using British pounds.

   a. If the Canadian manufacturer holds on to the British pounds, does NX = NFI in this case? Explain. _____
   _____
   _____

   b. Suppose the Canadian manufacturer uses the pounds to help build a factory in Great Britain. Does NX = NFI in this case? Explain. What kind of foreign investment is this? _____
   _____
   _____

   c. Suppose the Canadian manufacturer uses the pounds to buy stock in a British corporation. Does NX = NFI in this case? Explain. What kind of foreign investment is this? _____
   _____
   _____

   d. Suppose the Canadian manufacturer uses the pounds to buy computer chips manufactured in Great Britain. Does NX = NFI in this case? Explain. _____
   _____
   _____

3. Suppose the nominal exchange rate is 100 yen per dollar. Further, suppose the price of a tonne of Canadian corn is $5 and the price of a tonne of Japanese corn is 750 yen.

a. What is the real exchange rate between Japan and Canada in terms of corn?

_____

_____

_____

b. Does a dollar have purchasing-power parity in Canada and Japan? Explain.

_____

_____

_____

c. Is there a profit opportunity that you could exploit with arbitrage? Where would you buy and where would you sell?_____

_____

_____

d. If the nominal exchange rate stayed the same, what should happen to the price of corn in Canada and Japan? Explain. _____

_____

e. Suppose prices move as you have suggested in part (d). What has happened to the real exchange rate? _____

_____

_____

4. Suppose the price of Canadian-bottled spring water is $40 per case in Canada and 60 000 lira in Italy.

a. What is the nominal lira/dollar exchange rate if purchasing-power parity holds?

_____

_____

b. Suppose Italy's central bank is politically pressured to double its money supply which doubles the level of its prices. If purchasing-power parity holds, what is the new lira/dollar exchange rate? Did the lira appreciate or depreciate?

_____

_____

c. Suppose the Bank of Canada now doubles the Canadian money supply which doubles the level of Canadian prices. If purchasing-power parity holds, what is the value of the lira/dollar exchange rate? Did the dollar appreciate or depreciate?_____

_____

_____

d. Compare your answer to part (a) and part (c). What has happened to the exchange rate? Why? _____

_____

_____

E. Advanced Critical Thinking

You are watching a national news broadcast with your parents. The news anchor explains that the exchange rate for the dollar just hit its lowest value in a decade. The on-the-spot report shifts to a spokesman for Nortel Networks, a telecommunications equipment manufacturer. The spokesman reports that sales of its telecommunications equipment has hit an all-time high and so has the value of its stock. Your parents are shocked by the report's positive view of the low value of the dollar. They just cancelled their European vacation because of the dollar's low value.

1. Why do Nortel and your parents have different opinions about the value of the dollar? _____

_____

_____

_____

2. Nortel imports many parts for its manufacturing processes and it sells many finished products abroad. Since it is happy about a low dollar, what must be true about the amounts of Nortel's imports and exports? _____

_____

3. If someone argues that a strong dollar is "good for Canada" because Canadians are able to exchange some of their GDP for a greater amount of foreign GDP, is it true that a strong dollar is good for every Canadian? Why? _____

_____

_____

III. Solutions

A. True/False Questions

1. F; net exports are exports minus imports.
2. T
3. T
4. T
5. F; they are more likely to be traded because shipping costs are a small portion of the total cost of the good.
6. F; if exports exceed imports, the country has a trade surplus.
7. T
8. F; the exchange rate should be 90 yen/dollar.
9. T

10. F; the value of the lira should fall relative to the mark.
11. T
12. T
13. T
14. T
15. F; companies preferring a strong dollar import more than they export.

B. Multiple-Choice Questions

1. e	6. e	11. b	16. a
2. c	7. b	12. d	17. c
3. b	8. d	13. b	18. b
4. b	9. e	14. d	19. d
5. c	10. a	15. a	20. a

C. Short-Answer Questions

1. Improved transportation, advances in telecommunications, more valuable technologically advanced products, favourable government policies.

2. Purchase of foreign assets by domestic residents minus purchase of domestic assets by foreigners. NFI decreases.

3. Domestically (I) or foreign countries (NFI) because $S = I + NFI$.

4. Domestic investment grows because less national saving is allocated abroad, and/or more foreign saving is allocated here.

5. Pleased, because a strong dollar means they can buy imports cheaply and offer lower prices to their customers.

6. If Canadian prices fall, the foreign currency/dollar exchange rate falls, or the foreign price level rises, then Canadian goods are less expensive to foreigners.

7. $16 000 American/$20 000 Canadian = 0.80 American dollars per Canadian dollar. If $0.80 American = $1.00 Canadian, then $1.25 Canadian = $1.00 American.

8. Increase the accuracy because the greater the number of traded goods, the more accurate is purchasing-power parity.

9. It should rise because, in the long run, a higher rate of growth of money causes a higher rate of growth in prices. Lower inflation in Canada increases the relative value of its currency.

10. Because of higher default risk and higher tax rates in Canada.

D. Practice Problems

1. a. NFI rises. Foreign portfolio investment.

    b. Canadian NX falls and a Japanese manufacturer is holding Canadian dollars, therefore, NFI falls. Foreign portfolio investment.

    c. NFI falls. Foreign direct investment.

    d. NFI falls. Foreign portfolio investment.

    e. NFI rises. Foreign direct investment.

2. a. Yes, NX has risen by the size of the sale and NFI has risen an equal amount and is the size of the company's holdings of foreign currency.

    b. Yes, NX has risen by the size of the sale and NFI has risen an equal amount and is the size of the company's purchase of foreign capital. Foreign direct investment.

    c. Yes, NX has risen by the size of the sale and NFI has risen an equal amount and is the size of the company's purchase of foreign capital. Foreign portfolio investment.

    d. Yes, NX and NFI are both unchanged because exports rise by the same amount as imports, leaving NX unchanged. NFI was not involved.

3. a. $$\frac{100 \text{ yen/dollar} \times \$5/\text{Canadian tonne}}{750 \text{ yen/Japanese tonne}}$$

       = 0.67 Japanese tonne per Canadian tonne

    b. No, $1 buys $1/$5 tonne or 0.20 of a tonne of Canadian corn. $1 buys 100 yen and 100 yen buys 100/750 or 0.13 of a tonne of Japanese corn. (Or 1 tonne costs $5 in Canada and $7.50 in Japan.)

    c. Yes. Buy corn in Canada and sell it in Japan.

    d. The price should rise in Canada due to an increase in demand and fall in Japan due to an increase in supply.

    e. The real exchange rate will rise until it is equal to one (1 Japanese tonne to 1 Canadian tonne).

4. a. 60 000 lira/40 dollars = 1500 lira/dollar

   b. 120 000 lira/40 dollars = 3000 lira/dollar, depreciate

   c. 120 000 lira/80 dollars = 1500 lira/dollar, depreciate

   d. It is unchanged. When prices rise proportionally, it has no effect on the nominal exchange rate if purchasing-power parity holds.

E. Advanced Critical Thinking

1. Nortel sells much of its equipment to foreigners and the low value of the dollar makes Nortel's products inexpensive to foreigners. Your parents were going to buy foreign goods and services and the dollar cost became higher.

2. Nortel must sell a greater amount of products abroad than they purchase. That is, they are a net exporter.

3. No. A strong dollar benefits Canadians that are net importers and harms Canadians that are net exporters.

Chapter 13: A Macroeconomic Theory of the Open Economy

I. Chapter Overview

A. Context and Purpose

Chapter 13 is the second chapter in a two-chapter sequence on open economy macroeconomics. Chapter 12 explained the basic concepts and vocabulary associated with an open economy. Chapter 13 ties these concepts together into a theory of the open economy.

The purpose of Chapter 13 is to establish the interdependence of a number of economic variables in an open economy. In particular, Chapter 13 demonstrates the relationships between the prices and quantities in the market for loanable funds and the market for foreign-currency exchange. Using these markets, we can analyze the impact of a variety of economic events and government policies on an economy's exchange rate and trade balance.

B. Helpful Hints

1. *A change in national saving generates the same results regardless of whether the change was from private saving or public saving.* In your text there is a demonstration of the impact of an increase in a government budget deficit on an open economy. It is shown that an increase in a budget deficit causes a reduction in the public saving component of national saving that shifts the supply of loanable funds to the left. Note that a reduction in the private saving component of national saving also shifts the supply of loanable funds to the left. Thus, the example given in your text can be utilized for cases when there is a change in private saving. (The source of the change in saving will generate differences in the amount of output purchased by consumers versus government, but it will not alter any of the international analysis.)

2. *To find the change in NX (net exports), remember that NX = NFI (net foreign investment).* When we use our model to discover the impact of a government policy or an economic event on the economic variables in an open economy, there is no way to directly read net exports (the trade balance) from any of the graphs. However, the quantity of NFI is always directly measurable as the supply of dollars in the market for foreign-currency exchange. Since NFI = NX, whenever there is an increase in NFI, there is an equivalent increase in NX (which is an improvement in the trade balance). Whenever NFI declines, there is an equivalent decline in NX.

3. *Capital flight reduces domestic investment.* The discussion of capital flight in the text notes that capital flight increases net foreign investment and the supply of the domestic currency on the foreign-currency exchange market which lowers the exchange value of the domestic currency. Since these activities raise net exports (improve the trade balance) why is capital flight considered bad for the economy rather than good? Look at panel (a) of Figure 13-7 of your text. Since borrowers

must now pay a higher interest rate than they paid before the crisis of confidence, the quantity of loanable funds demanded for domestic investment falls. Domestic investment is reduced by an amount equal to the increase in net exports. Capital flight, therefore, reduces domestic investment and, with it, the prospect for long-term economic growth in the country.

4. *Work the examples in the text backward.* The examples demonstrated in your text require a significant degree of concentration to understand. Once you have mastered them, you should feel comfortable that you can follow someone else's demonstration. The next step is to work those same examples backward, alone. (See Practice Problem #1) That is, address the effect of a decrease in the world interest rate, a reduction in the budget deficit, the lowering of a trade restriction, and the effect of capital inflow.

II. Self-Testing Challenge

A. True/False Questions

_____1.   Net foreign investment is the purchase of domestic assets by foreigners minus the purchase of foreign assets by domestic residents.

_____2.   A country's net foreign investment (NFI) is always equal to its net exports (NX).

_____3.   Other things being the same, an increase in the world's real interest rate increases net foreign investment for a small open economy.

_____4.   An increase in Canadian net foreign investment increases the supply of dollars in the market for foreign-currency exchange and decreases the real exchange rate of the dollar.

_____5.   If labour unions convince Canadians to "buy Canadian," it will improve the Canadian trade balance.

_____6.   Net foreign investment is negative when domestic investment exceeds national saving at the world interest rate.

_____7.   An increase in the government's budget deficit shifts the supply of loanable funds to the right.

_____8.   An increase in the government's budget deficit tends to cause the real exchange rate of the dollar to depreciate.

_____9.   Data for the Canadian economy show that the rise in government deficits over the 1975-95 period reduced net exports.

_____10.   If Canada raises its tariff on imported wine, it will reduce imports and improve the trade balance.

_____11.   If Canada raises its tariff on imported wine, domestic wine producers will benefit, but the dollar will appreciate and domestic producers of export goods will be harmed.

_____12. An increase in the government budget deficit causes the real exchange rate to appreciate.

_____13. A country experiencing capital flight will experience a reduction in its net foreign investment and its net exports.

_____14. If Canadians increase their saving, the dollar will appreciate in the market for foreign-currency exchange.

_____15. A rise in Mexico's net exports (NX) will increase the demand for pesos in the market for foreign-currency exchange and the peso will appreciate in value.

B. Multiple-Choice Questions

1. Which of the following statements regarding the loanable funds market in a small open economy is not true?
   a. The real interest rate is equal to the world real interest rate.
   b. Net foreign investment is positive when the demand for loanable funds exceeds the supply of loanable funds at the world interest rate.
   c. Domestic investment determines the demand for loanable funds.
   d. National saving determines the supply of loanable funds.
   e. All of the above are true.

2. An increase in the government budget deficit
   a. reduces net foreign investment.
   b. causes the real exchange rate to depreciate.
   c. increases net exports.
   d. increases the demand for loanable funds.
   e. causes none of the above.

3. Which of the following statements regarding the loanable funds market is true?
   a. An increase in private saving shifts the supply of loanable funds to the left.
   b. A decrease in the government budget deficit decreases national saving.
   c. An increase in the government budget deficit shifts the supply of loanable funds to the right.
   d. An increase in the government budget deficit shifts the supply of loanable funds to the left.

4. Other things being equal, a higher world real interest rate
   a. causes the Canadian dollar to appreciate.
   b. increases Canadian net foreign investment.
   c. increases the quantity demanded of loanable funds for domestic investment.
   d. decreases the quantity supplied of loanable funds from national saving.

5. An increase in Europe's taste for Canadian-produced wine would cause the dollar to
   a. depreciate and would increase Canadian net exports.
   b. depreciate and would decrease Canadian net exports.
   c. appreciate and would increase Canadian net exports.
   d. appreciate and would decrease Canadian net exports.
   e. appreciate, but the total value of Canadian net export stays the same.

6. A decrease in the federal government budget deficit
   a. increases Canadian net exports and decreases Canadian net foreign investment.
   b. decreases Canadian net exports and increases Canadian net foreign investment.
   c. decreases Canadian net exports and Canadian net foreign investment the same amount.
   d. increases Canadian net exports and Canadian net foreign investment the same amount.

7. An increase in the government budget deficit results in all of the following except
   a. a fall in public saving.
   b. a fall in national saving.
   c. a rise in domestic investment.
   d. a fall in net foreign investment.

8. Which of the following statements regarding the market for foreign-currency exchange is true?
   a. An increase in Canadian net exports increases the supply of dollars and the dollar depreciates.
   b. An increase in Canadian net exports decreases the supply of dollars and the dollar depreciates.
   c. An increase in Canadian net exports decreases the demand for dollars and the dollar appreciates.
   d. An increase in Canadian net exports increases the demand for dollars and the dollar appreciates.

9. Which of the following statements regarding the market for foreign-currency exchange is true?
   a. An increase in Canadian net foreign investment increases the supply of dollars and the dollar appreciates.
   b. An increase in Canadian net foreign investment increases the supply of dollars and the dollar depreciates.
   c. An increase in Canadian net foreign investment increases the demand for dollars and the dollar appreciates.
   d. An increase in Canadian net foreign investment increases the demand for dollars and the dollar depreciates.

10. If Canada imposes a quota on the importing of apparel produced in China, which of the following is true regarding the market for foreign-currency exchange?
    a. The supply of dollars increases and the dollar depreciates.
    b. The supply of dollars decreases and the dollar appreciates.
    c. The demand for dollars increases and the dollar appreciates.
    d. The demand for dollars decreases and the dollar depreciates.

11. If Canada imposes a quota on the importing of apparel produced in China, which of the following is true regarding Canadian net exports?
    a. Net exports will rise.
    b. Net exports will fall.
    c. Net exports will remain unchanged.

12. Suppose, due to political instability, Mexicans suddenly choose to invest in Canadian assets as opposed to Mexican assets. Which of the following statements is true regarding Canadian net foreign investment?
    a. Canadian net foreign investment rises.
    b. Canadian net foreign investment falls.
    c. Canadian net foreign investment is unchanged because only Canadian residents can alter Canadian net foreign investment.

13. Suppose, due to political instability, Mexicans suddenly choose to invest in Canadian assets as opposed to Mexican assets. Which of the following statements is true regarding the value of the dollar and Canadian net exports?
    a. The dollar appreciates and Canadian net exports fall.
    b. The dollar depreciates and Canadian net exports fall.
    c. The dollar appreciates and Canadian net exports rise.
    d. The dollar depreciates and Canadian net exports rise.

14. An increase in Canadian private saving
    a. increases Canadian net exports and decreases Canadian net foreign investment.
    b. decreases Canadian net exports and increases Canadian net foreign investment.
    c. decreases Canadian net exports and Canadian net foreign investment the same amount.
    d. increases Canadian net exports and Canadian net foreign investment the same amount.

15. Which of the following statements about trade policy is true?
    a. A restrictive import quota increases a country's net exports.
    b. A restrictive import quota decreases a country's net exports.
    c. A country's trade policy has no impact on the size of its trade balance.
    d. None of the above.

16. Which of the following groups would *not* benefit from a Canadian import quota on Japanese autos?
    a. stockholders of Canadian auto manufacturers
    b. Canadian farmers who export grain
    c. members of the Canadian Auto Workers union
    d. Canadian consumers who buy electronics from Japan

17. An example of a trade policy is
    a. an increase in the government budget deficit because it reduces a country's net exports.
    b. capital flight because it increases a country's net exports.
    c. a tariff on footwear.
    d. all of the above.

18. An export subsidy should have the same effect on the exchange rate as
    a. a tariff.
    b. capital flight.
    c. a decrease in the government budget deficit.
    d. an increase in private saving.

19. Which of the following groups would be most harmed by a Canadian government budget deficit?
    a. Canadian residents wishing to buy foreign-produced autos
    b. borrowers of loanable funds
    c. Canadians who wish to travel abroad
    d. Molson selling beer to the U.S.

20. Capital flight
    a. decreases a country's net exports and increases its long-run growth path.
    b. decreases a country's net exports and decreases its long-run growth path.
    c. increases a country's net exports and decreases its long-run growth path.
    d. increases a country's net exports and increases its long-run growth path.

C. Short-Answer Questions

1. How is net foreign investment determined in a small open economy with perfect capital mobility? _____

   _____

   _____

2. Explain the source of the supply of dollars in the market for foreign-currency exchange. _____

   _____

   _____

3. Explain the source of the demand for dollars in the market for foreign-currency exchange. _____
_____
_____

4. Why might certain companies and unions support tariffs and import quotas even if they know that these restrictions cannot alter the trade balance? _____
_____
_____
_____

5. Suppose the quality of Canadian goods and services falls and, as a result, foreigners choose to buy fewer Canadian goods. Does this affect the Canadian balance of trade? Why? _____
_____
_____
_____

6. What happens to the value of a country's currency if there is capital flight from that country? Explain. _____
_____
_____
_____

7. What would an increase in the saving of Canadian residents do to the Canadian trade balance and the dollar exchange rate? Explain. _____
_____
_____
_____

8. Why are budget deficits and trade deficits related to each other? _____
_____
_____
_____

9. Do trade restrictions (such as tariffs and import quotas) alter NX? _____
_____
_____
_____

D. Practice Problems

1. This problem is composed from the examples in the chapter except the source of the change has been reversed. Use the model in the textbook to answer the following questions.

a. Suppose there is a decrease in the world interest rate. Describe the sequence of events in the model by describing the shifts in the curves and discuss the movements in the relevant macroeconomic variables. _____

_____

_____

_____

b. Suppose the government reduces its budget deficit. Describe the sequence of events in the model by describing the shifts in the curves and discuss the movements in the relevant macroeconomic variables. _____

_____

_____

_____

c. Suppose the government reduces a quota on the importing of Japanese automobiles. Describe the sequence of events in the model by describing the shifts in the curves and discuss the movements in the relevant macroeconomic variables. _____

_____

_____

_____

d. Suppose the perceived risk of holding Mexican assets disappears, and borrowers in Mexico can pay the world interest rate. Describe the sequence of events in the model by describing the shifts in the curves and discuss the movements in the relevant macroeconomic variables. _____

_____

_____

_____

2. a. Suppose private saving increased at each real interest rate. What would happen to the important macroeconomic variables in our model of an open economy?

_____

_____

_____

_____

b. Is there any difference between your answer above and the answer you would write if the government had reduced its deficit? Why? _____

_____

_____

c. Suppose the government passes an investment tax credit that increases domestic investment at each real interest rate. How would this change the important economic variables in the model? _____

_____

_____

_____

d. Compare your answer in part (a) (an increase in saving at each real interest rate) to your answer in part (c) (an increase in domestic investment at each real interest rate). Are there any differences? _____

_____

_____

3. Suppose Canadian preferences for Japanese automobiles increase.

a. What happens to the demand for dollars in the foreign-currency exchange market? _____

_____

b. What happens to the value of the dollar in the foreign-currency exchange market? _____

_____

_____

c. What happens to Canadian net exports? Why? _____

_____

d. If Canada is importing more cars, what must be true about Canadian imports and exports of other items? _____

_____

_____

4. Suppose Canada is perceived to be politically unstable and this induces capital flight to the U.S.

a. Describe what happens in the foreign-currency exchange market from the perspective of Canada. _____

_____

_____

b. Describe what happens in the foreign-currency exchange market from the perspective of the U.S. _____

_____

_____

c. Are your answers to part (a) and (b) above consistent with one another? Why?

_____

_____

_____

d. What should this event do to each country's balance of trade? _____

_____

_____

_____

e. Which country will tend to grow faster in the future? Why? _____

_____

_____

_____

E. Advanced Critical Thinking

Hong Kong has a capitalist economic system. It was leased from China by Great Britain for 100 years. In 1997, it was returned to China, a socialist republic.

1. What do you think happened to the net foreign investment of Hong Kong from 1990 to 1997? Why? _____

_____

_____

_____

2. The residents of Hong Kong have chosen Canada, particularly the Vancouver area, as a place to move some of their business activity. What impact do you suppose this has had on Canada's net foreign investment, net exports, and exchange rate? _____

_____

_____

_____

3. Which Canadian industries, those engaged in importing or exporting, are likely to be pleased with Hong Kong's investment in Canada? Why? _____

_____

_____

_____

4. What impact will Hong Kong's return to China have on the growth rate of Canada?

_____

_____

_____

_____

III. Solutions

A. True/False Questions

1. F; NFI is the purchase of foreign assets by domestic residents minus the purchase of domestic assets by foreigners.
2. T
3. T
4. T
5. F; net exports are unchanged because NFI is unchanged.
6. T
7. F; an increase in the government's budget deficit shifts the supply of loanable funds to the left.
8. F; an increase in the government's budget deficit raises the real exchange rate.
9. T
10. F; net exports are unchanged because NFI is unchanged.
11. T
12. T
13. F; a country experiencing capital flight will experience an increase in its NFI and its net exports.
14. F; the dollar will depreciate.
15. T

B. Multiple-Choice Questions

1. b	6. d	11. c	16. b
2. a	7. c	12. b	17. c
3. d	8. d	13. a	18. a
4. b	9. b	14. d	19. d
5. e	10. c	15. c	20. c

C. Short-Answer Questions

1. NFI is determined by the difference between the supply of loanable funds (national saving) and the demand for loanable funds (domestic investment) at the world interest rate.

2. It comes from dollars Canadians use for NFI.

3. It comes from the need for dollars from foreigners purchasing Canadian NX.

4. Because trade restrictions can improve the sales of some domestic companies facing competition from imports, but largely at the expense of other domestic companies producing for export.

5. No, it reduces the demand for dollars in the market for foreign-currency exchange and lowers the value of the dollar to keep NX unchanged.

6. It increases the supply of their currency in the market for foreign-currency exchange and lowers the exchange rate.

7. It increases NFI, increases the supply of dollars on the foreign-currency exchange market, lowers the dollar exchange rate, and increases NX.

8. Because a budget deficit reduces national saving, net foreign investment, and net exports.

9. Trade restrictions don't alter the total value of NX because NX = NFI. However, trade restrictions alter the composition of NX.

D. Practice Problems

1. a. A decrease in the world interest rate reduces the quantity supplied of loanable funds and increases the quantity demanded of loanable funds. As a result, net foreign investment decreases, which, in turn, shifts the supply-of-dollars curve in the foreign exchange market to the left. The real exchange rate appreciates, causing net exports to fall.

    b. A decrease in the government budget deficit increases national saving, which shifts the supply-of-loanable-funds curve to the right. Net foreign investment increases, which, in turn, shifts the supply-of-dollars curve in the foreign exchange market to the right. The real exchange rate depreciates, causing net exports to rise.

    c. A reduction in an import quota has no impact in the market for loanable funds. Net foreign investment is not affected, so the supply-of-dollars curve in the foreign exchange market does not shift. The demand-for-dollars curve shifts to the left, causing the real exchange rate to depreciate. No change in the trade balance, but a higher volume of trade (more imports and more exports).

    d. With no risk premium, the interest rate paid on Mexican assets is the world interest rate. The supply-of-loanable-funds curve shifts down, leaving the quantity supplied of loanable funds unchanged. The quantity demanded of loanable funds increases, resulting in a fall in net foreign investment. The supply-of-pesos curve in the foreign exchange market shifts to the left, which causes the real exchange rate to appreciate and net exports to fall.

2. a. Supply of loanable funds shifts right, NFI increases, increasing the supply of dollars in the foreign-currency exchange market, which causes the real exchange rate to depreciate and net exports to rise.

    b. No, because it doesn't matter why national saving increased. Either one will shift the supply of loanable funds to the right.

c. Increase in the demand for loanable funds, lowers NFI, decreases the supply of dollars in the foreign-currency exchange market, which causes the real exchange rate to appreciate and net exports to fall.

d. An increase in saving moves the trade balance toward surplus, while an increase in investment demand moves it toward deficit.

3. a. Shifts left.

b. Real exchange rate falls so the value of the dollar falls.

c. NFI is unchanged, therefore, NX as a total is unchanged.

d. If NX is constant, Canada must be importing less or exporting more of other items.

4. a. The supply of Canadian dollars shifts right and the value of the Canadian dollar falls.

b. The supply of U.S. dollars shifts left and the value of the U.S. dollar rises.

c. Yes. A rise in the value of the U.S. dollar relative to the Canadian dollar should correspond to the fall in the value of the Canadian dollar relative to the U.S. dollar.

d. The fall in the value of the Canadian dollar will improve NX, while the stronger U.S. dollar will lower NX by the U.S.

e. Canada is increasing its NFI in the U.S. and the U.S. is decreasing its NFI in Canada, so the U.S. will likely grow faster.

E. Advanced Critical Thinking

1. The NFI of Hong Kong has increased because foreigners are not buying assets in Hong Kong and Hong Kong residents are buying assets abroad — capital flight. Investors fear China will nationalize much of Hong Kong's industry.

2. This has decreased Canada's NFI. The reduced NFI reduces the supply of Canadian dollars in the foreign-currency exchange market, raises the exchange rate, and lowers net exports.

3. The increase in the value of the Canadian dollar has made Canadian producers less competitive abroad, but has made imports cheaper. Thus, exporters have been hurt, while companies that import are better off.

4. The reduction in Canada's NFI (due to Hong Kong's increased NFI) increases the capital stock of Canada causing it to grow.

Chapter 14: Aggregate Demand and Aggregate Supply

I. Chapter Overview

A. Context and Purpose

To this point, our study of macroeconomic theory has concentrated on the behaviour of the economy in the long run. Chapters 14-16 now focus on short-run fluctuations in the economy around its long-run trend. Chapter 14 introduces aggregate demand and aggregate supply and shows how shifts in these curves can cause recessions. Chapter 15 focuses on how policymakers use the tools of monetary and fiscal policy to influence aggregate demand. Chapter 16 addresses the short-run relationship between inflation and unemployment.

The purpose of Chapter 14 is to develop the model economists use to analyze the economy's short-run fluctuations — the model of aggregate demand and aggregate supply. We will learn about the sources for shifts in the aggregate-demand curve and the aggregate-supply curve and how these shifts can cause recessions. We will also introduce actions policymakers might undertake to offset recessions.

B. Helpful Hints

1. *There are no changes in real variables along the long-run aggregate-supply curve.* When all prices change equally, no real variables have changed. A vertical long-run aggregate-supply curve demonstrates this classic lesson. Pick any point on the long-run aggregate-supply curve. Now double the price level and all nominal values, such as, wages. Although the price level has doubled, relative prices have remained constant including the real wage, W/P. There has been no change in anyone's incentive to produce and, thus, no change in output. It follows that if the economy is temporarily producing a level of output other than the long-run natural level, then at least some wages or prices have failed to adjust to the long-run equilibrium price level causing at least some relative prices to change so as to stimulate or discourage production. This is, in fact, what is happening along a short-run aggregate-supply curve.

2. *Output can fluctuate to levels both above and below the natural level of output.* The examples of economic fluctuations in the text focus on recessions. That is, the examples deal with periods when output is less than the natural level. Note, however, that output can be above the natural level temporarily because unemployment can be below its natural rate. This will occur when there is a positive aggregate demand shock — for example, if there is an increase in the money supply or an increase in domestic investment. It will also occur if there is a positive aggregate supply shock — for example, if the price of oil were to fall or union wage demands were to decrease. To help you, these cases are addressed in the problems that follow.

3. *Tables 14-1 and 14-2 in the textbook provide a very useful summary of the aggregate-demand and aggregate-supply curves.*

The textbook explains that an increase in the expected price level shifts the short-run aggregate-supply curve to the left. It is helpful to remember that such shifts often are caused by increases in production costs, such as higher nominal wages or higher natural resource prices.

II. Self-Testing Challenges

When necessary, draw a graph of the model of aggregate demand and aggregate supply on scratch paper to help you answer the following problems and questions.

A. True/False Questions

_____1. Over the last 100 years, Canadian real GDP has grown on average at about 2% per year.

_____2. Investment is a particularly volatile component of spending across the business cycle.

_____3. When real GDP declines, the unemployment rate also declines.

_____4. If the classical dichotomy and monetary neutrality hold in the long run, then the long-run aggregate-supply curve should be vertical.

_____5. Economists refer to fluctuations in output as the "business cycle" because movements in output are regular and predictable.

_____6. One reason aggregate demand slopes downward is the wealth effect: a decrease in the price level increases the value of money holdings and consumer spending rises.

_____7. If the Bank of Canada increases the money supply, the aggregate-demand curve shifts to the left.

_____8. The misperceptions theory explains why the long-run aggregate-supply curve is vertical.

_____9. A rise in price expectations that causes wages to rise causes the short-run aggregate-supply curve to shift left.

_____10. If the economy is in a recession, the economy will adjust to long-run equilibrium on its own as wages and price expectations rise.

_____11. In the short run, if the government cuts back spending to balance its budget, it may cause a recession.

_____12. The short-run effect of an increase in aggregate demand is an increase in output and an increase in the price level.

_____13. A rise in the price of oil tends to cause stagflation.

_____14. In the long run, an increase in government spending tends to increase output and prices.

_____15. If policymakers choose to try to move the economy out of a recession, they should use their policy tools to decrease aggregate demand.

B. Multiple-Choice Questions

1. Which of the following statements about economic fluctuations is true?
   a. A recession is when output rises above the natural level of output.
   b. A depression is a mild recession.
   c. Economic fluctuations have been termed the "business cycle" because the movements in output are regular and predictable.
   d. A variety of spending, income, and output measures can be used to measure economic fluctuations because most macroeconomic quantities tend to fluctuate together.
   e. None of the above.

2. Which if the following would shift the aggregate-demand curve to the right?
   a. a decrease in government spending on highways
   b. a cut in personal income taxes
   c. an exchange rate appreciation
   d. a rise in interest rates

3. Which of the following would shift the aggregate-demand curve to the left?
   a. a boom in the stock market
   b. a fall in interest rates
   c. an exchange rate depreciation
   d. a fall in expected future profits by firms

4. Which of the following is *not* a reason why the aggregate-demand curve slopes downward?
   a. the wealth effect
   b. the interest-rate effect
   c. the classical dichotomy/monetary neutrality effects
   d. the real exchange rate effect
   e. none of the above

5. In the model of aggregate supply and aggregate demand, the initial impact of an increase in consumer optimism is to
   a. shift short-run aggregate supply to the right.
   b. shift short-run aggregate supply to the left.
   c. shift aggregate demand to the right.
   d. shift aggregate demand to the left.
   e. shift long-run aggregate supply to the left.

6. Which of the following statements is true regarding the long-run aggregate-supply curve? The long-run aggregate-supply curve
   a. shifts left when the natural rate of unemployment falls.
   b. is vertical because an equal change in all prices and wages leaves output unaffected.
   c. is positively sloped because price expectations and wages tend to be fixed in the long run.
   d. shifts right when the government raises the minimum wage.

7. According to the wealth effect, aggregate demand slopes downward (negatively) because
   a. lower prices increase the value of money holdings and consumer spending increases.
   b. lower prices decrease the value of money holdings and consumer spending decreases.
   c. lower prices reduce money holdings, increase lending, interest rates fall, and investment spending increases.
   d. lower prices increase money holdings, decrease lending, interest rates rise, and investment spending falls.

8. The natural level of output is the amount of real GDP produced
   a. when there is no unemployment.
   b. when the economy is at the natural rate of investment.
   c. when the economy is at the natural rate of aggregate demand.
   d. when the economy is at the natural rate of unemployment.

9. Suppose the price level falls, but because of fixed nominal wage contracts, the real wage rises and firms cut back on production. This is a demonstration of
   a. the misperceptions theory of the short-run aggregate-supply curve.
   b. the sticky-wage theory of the short-run aggregate-supply curve.
   c. the sticky-price theory of the short-run aggregate-supply curve.
   d. the classical dichotomy theory of the short-run aggregate-supply curve.

10. Suppose the price level falls but suppliers only notice that the price of their particular product has fallen. Thinking there has been a fall in the relative price of their product, they cut back on production. This is a demonstration of
    a. the misperceptions theory of the short-run aggregate-supply curve.
    b. the sticky-wage theory of the short-run aggregate-supply curve.
    c. the sticky-price theory of the short-run aggregate-supply curve.
    d. the classical dichotomy theory of the short-run aggregate-supply curve.

11. Suppose the economy is initially in long-run equilibrium. Then suppose there is
    a reduction in government spending on infrastructure projects. According to the
    model of aggregate demand and aggregate supply, what happens to prices and
    output in the *short run*?
    a. prices rise, output rises
    b. prices rise, output falls
    c. prices fall, output falls
    d. prices fall, output rises

12. Suppose the economy is initially in long-run equilibrium. Then suppose there is
    a reduction in government spending on infrastructure projects. According to the
    model of aggregate demand and aggregate supply, what happens to prices and
    output in the *long run*?
    a. prices rise, output is unchanged from its initial value
    b. prices fall, output is unchanged from its initial value
    c. output rises, prices are unchanged from the initial value
    d. output falls, prices are unchanged from the initial value
    e. output and the price level are unchanged from their initial values

13. Suppose the economy is initially in long-run equilibrium. Then suppose there is a
    drought that destroys much of the wheat crop. According to the model of aggregate
    demand and aggregate supply, what happens to prices and output in the *short run*?
    a. prices rise, output rises
    b. prices rise, output falls
    c. prices fall, output falls
    d. prices fall, output rises

14. Suppose the economy is initially in long-run equilibrium. Then suppose there is
    a drought that destroys much of the wheat crop. If the policymakers allow the
    economy to adjust to long-run equilibrium on its own, according to the model of
    aggregate demand and aggregate supply, what happens to prices and output in the
    long run?
    a. prices rise, output is unchanged from its initial value
    b. prices fall, output is unchanged from its initial value
    c. output rises, prices are unchanged from the initial value
    d. output falls, prices are unchanged from the initial value
    e. output and the price level are unchanged from their initial values

15. Stagflation occurs when there are
    a. falling prices and falling output.
    b. falling prices and rising output.
    c. rising prices and rising output.
    d. rising prices and falling output.

16. The initial impact of which of the following events is a shift in the short-run aggregate-supply curve to the right?
    a. an increase in government spending on military equipment
    b. an increase in price expectations
    c. a drop in oil prices
    d. a decrease in the money supply
    e. none of the above

17. Suppose the economy is operating in a recession. If policymakers wished to move output to its long-run natural level, they should attempt to
    a. shift aggregate demand to the right.
    b. shift aggregate demand to the left.
    c. shift short-run aggregate supply to the right.
    d. shift short-run aggregate supply to the left.

18. Suppose the economy is operating in a recession. If policymakers allow the economy to adjust to the long-run natural level on its own,
    a. people will raise their price expectations and the short-run aggregate supply will shift left.
    b. people will reduce their price expectations and the short-run aggregate supply will shift right.
    c. people will raise their price expectations and aggregate demand will shift left.
    d. people will reduce their price expectations and aggregate demand will shift right.

19. According to the model of aggregate supply and aggregate demand, in the long run, an increase in the money supply should cause
    a. prices to rise and output to rise.
    b. prices to fall and output to fall.
    c. prices to rise and output to remain unchanged.
    d. prices to fall and output to remain unchanged.

20. Policymakers are said to "accommodate" an adverse supply shock if they
    a. respond to the adverse supply shock by increasing aggregate demand which further raises prices.
    b. respond to the adverse supply shock by decreasing aggregate demand which lowers prices.
    c. respond to the adverse supply shock by decreasing short-run aggregate supply.
    d. fail to respond to the adverse supply shock and allow the economy to adjust on its own.

C. Short-Answer Questions

1. Name the three key facts about economic fluctuations. _____

_____

_____

2. Which component of aggregate demand varies the most over the business cycle?

_____

3. What happens to the natural level of output when the natural rate of unemployment falls? _____

_____

4. What are the three reasons the aggregate-demand curve slopes downward? Explain them. _____

_____

_____

_____

_____

_____

_____

5. Suppose the economy is in long-run equilibrium. If we employ the sticky-wage theory of the short-run aggregate-supply curve, what initially happens to the real wage if there is a decrease in aggregate demand? _____

_____

_____

6. Referring to question 5, if the economy is to adjust on its own back to the long-run equilibrium level of output, what must happen to the real wage?_____

_____

_____

7. If the economy is in a recession, why might policymakers choose to adjust aggregate demand to eliminate the recession rather then let the economy adjust, or self-correct, on its own?_____

_____

_____

8. Does a shift in aggregate demand alter output in the long run? Why?_____

_____

_____

_____

9. Why is money unlikely to be neutral in the short run? _____

_____

_____

_____

10. Suppose OPEC breaks apart and oil prices fall substantially. Initially, which curve shifts in the aggregate-supply/aggregate-demand model? In what direction does it shift? What happens to the price level and real output? _____

_____

_____

D. Practice Problems

1. For the following four cases, trace the impact of each shock in the aggregate-supply aggregate-demand model by answering the following three questions for each: What happens to prices and output in the short run? What happens to prices and output in the long run if the economy is allowed to adjust to long-run equilibrium on its own? If policymakers had intervened to move output back to the natural level instead of allowing the economy to self-correct, in which direction should they have moved aggregate demand?

   a. aggregate demand shifts left _____

   _____

   _____

   b. aggregate demand shifts right _____

   _____

   _____

   c. short-run aggregate supply shifts left _____

   _____

   _____

   d. short-run aggregate supply shifts right _____

   _____

   _____

2. The following events have their *initial impact* on which of the following: aggregate demand, long-run aggregate supply, or short-run aggregate supply? Does the curve shift to the right or left?

   a. The government repairs aging roads and bridges. _____

   _____

   b. OPEC raises oil prices. _____

   c. The government raises Employment Insurance benefits. _____

   _____

   d. Canadians feel more secure in their jobs and become more optimistic. _____

   _____

e. A technological advance takes place in the application of computers to the manufacture of steel. _____

f. The government increases the minimum wage. _____

g. Wage demands of new university graduates fall. _____

h. The Bank of Canada decreases the money supply. _____

i. A drought destroys much of the corn crop. _____

3. Suppose the economy is in long-run equilibrium. Then, suppose the Bank of Canada suddenly increases the money supply.

    a. Describe the initial impact of this event in the model of aggregate demand and aggregate supply by explaining which curve shifts which way. _____
_____
_____

    b. What happens to the price level and real output in the short run? _____
_____
_____

    c. If the economy is allowed to adjust to the increase in the money supply, what happens to the price level and real output in the long run? (compared to their original levels) _____
_____

    d. Does an increase in the money supply move output above the natural level indefinitely? Why? _____
_____
_____

4. Suppose the economy is in long-run equilibrium. Then, suppose workers and firms suddenly expect higher prices in the future and agree to an increase in wages.

    a. Describe the initial impact of this event in the model of aggregate demand and aggregate supply by explaining which curve shifts which way. _____
_____
_____

    b. What happens to the price level and real output in the short run? _____
_____

    c. What name do we have for this combination of movements in output and prices? _____

d. If policymakers wanted to move output back to the natural level of output, what should they do? _____
_____

e. If policymakers were able to move output back to the natural level of output, what would the policy do to prices? _____
_____

f. If policymakers did nothing at all, what would happen to the wage rate as the economy self-corrects or adjusts back to the natural level of output on its own?
_____
_____

g. Is it likely that an increase in price expectations and wages alone can cause a permanent increase in the price level? Why? _____
_____
_____

5. Suppose aggregate demand has decreased and the economy is in a recession. Describe the adjustment process necessary for the economy to adjust on its own to the natural level of output for each of the three theoretical short-run aggregate-supply curves.

a. The misperceptions theory: _____
_____
_____
_____
_____

b. The sticky-wage theory: _____
_____
_____
_____
_____

c. The sticky-price theory: _____
_____
_____
_____
_____

d. Do you think the type of adjustments described above would take place more quickly from a recession or from a period when output was above the long-run natural level? Why? _____
_____
_____

E. Advanced Critical Thinking

You are watching the evening news on television. The news anchor reports that union wage demands are much higher this year because the workers anticipate an increase in the rate of inflation. Your roommate says, "Inflation is a self-fulfilling prophecy. If workers think there are going to be higher prices, they demand higher wages. This increases the cost of production and firms raise their prices. Expecting higher prices simply causes higher prices."

1. Is this true in the short run? Explain. _____
    _____
    _____
    _____

2. If policymakers do nothing and allow the economy to adjust to the natural level of output on its own, does expecting higher prices cause higher prices in the long run? Explain. _____
    _____
    _____

3. If policymakers accommodate the adverse supply shock, does the expectation of higher prices cause higher prices in the long run? Explain. _____
    _____
    _____

III. Solutions

A. True/False Questions

1. F; the Canadian economy has grown on average at about 4% per year.
2. T
3. F; as output falls, unemployment rises.
4. T
5. F; fluctuations in output are irregular and unpredictable.
6. T
7. F; aggregate demand shifts to the right.
8. F; it explains why the short-run aggregate-supply curve is upward sloping.
9. T
10. F; in a recession, the economy adjusts to long-run equilibrium as wages and prices fall.
11. T
12. T
13. T
14. F; in the long run, it tends to increase prices, but it has no impact on output.
15. F; policymakers should increase aggregate demand.

B. Multiple-Choice Questions

1. d	6. b	11. c	16. c
2. b	7. a	12. b	17. a
3. d	8. d	13. b	18. b
4. c	9. b	14. e	19. c
5. c	10. a	15. d	20. a

C. Short-Answer Questions

1. Economic fluctuations are irregular and unpredictable, most macroeconomic quantities fluctuate together, and when output falls, unemployment rises.

2. Investment spending.

3. A fall in the natural rate of unemployment would increase the natural level of output, and shift the long-run aggregate-supply curve to the right.

4. Wealth effect: lower prices increase the value of money holdings and consumer spending increases. Interest rate effect: lower prices reduces the quantity of money held, some is loaned, interest rates fall, and investment spending increases. Real exchange rate effect: lower prices decrease the real exchange rate, and net exports increase.

5. Since the nominal wage is fixed for a period, the fall in the price level raises the real wage, W/P.

6. The nominal wage must fall so that the real wage can return to its initial level.

7. Because they think they can get the economy back to the long-run natural level of output more quickly or, in the case of a negative supply shock, because they are more concerned with output and employment than inflation.

8. No. In the long run, output is determined by factor supplies and technology (long-run aggregate supply). Changes in aggregate demand only affect output in the short run because it temporarily alters relative prices.

9. Because a shift in aggregate demand arising from a change in the money supply may change the price level unexpectedly. Some prices and wages adjust to the change in the price level more quickly than others causing changes in relative prices in the short run.

10. Short-run aggregate supply shifts right. Prices fall and output rises in the short run.

D. Practice Problems

1. a. Prices fall, output falls. Prices fall, output returns to the natural level. Shift aggregate demand to the right.

   b. Prices rise, output rises. Prices rise, output returns to the natural level. Shift aggregate demand to the left.

   c. Prices rise, output falls. Price level returns to original value, output returns to the natural level. Shift aggregate demand to the right.

   d. Prices fall, output rises. Price level returns to original value, output returns to the natural level. Shift aggregate demand to the left.

2. a. aggregate demand, right

   b. short-run aggregate supply, left

   c. short-run and long-run aggregate supply, left

   d. aggregate demand, right

   e. short-run and long-run aggregate supply, right

   f. short-run and long-run aggregate supply, left

   g. short-run aggregate supply, right

   h. aggregate demand, left

   i. short-run aggregate supply, left

3. a. Aggregate demand shifts to the right.

   b. Price level rises and real output rises.

   c. Price level rises and real output stays the same.

   d. No. Over time, people and firms adjust to the new higher amount of spending by raising their prices and wages.

4. a.   Short-run aggregate supply shifts left.

   b.   Prices rise and output falls.

   c.   Stagflation.

   d.   Shift aggregate demand to the right.

   e.   Prices would rise more and remain there.

   f.   The high unemployment at the low level of output would put pressure on the wage to fall back to its original value.

   g.   No. Increases in the cost of production need to be "accommodated" by government policy to permanently raise prices.

5. a.   Some firms mistakenly believe that only the price of their product has fallen and they cut back on production. As they realize that all prices are falling, they will increase production at each price, which will shift short-run aggregate supply to the right.

   b.   Nominal wage contracts are based on the expectation of a higher price level so the real wage has risen and workers were laid off. As workers and firms recognize the fall in the price level, new contracts will have a lower nominal wage, the real wage falls, and firms increase production at each price level shifting the short-run aggregate supply to the right.

   c.   Some firms have not reduced their prices because of menu costs. Their products are relatively more expensive and sales fall. When they realize the lower price level is permanent they lower their prices and production rises at each price level, shifting the short-run aggregate supply to the right.

   d.   More slowly from a recession because the adjustment requires prices and wages be reduced, and they are usually more sticky downward. The adjustment when output is above normal requires that prices and wages rise.

E. Advanced Critical Thinking

1. Yes. An increase in price expectations shifts the short-run aggregate-supply curve to the left and prices rise.

2. No. In the long run, the increase in unemployment will cause wages and price expectations to fall back to their prior levels.

3. Yes. If policymakers accommodate the adverse supply shock with an increase in aggregate demand, the price level will rise permanently.

Chapter 15: The Influence of Monetary and Fiscal Policy on Aggregate Demand

I. Chapter Overview

A. Context and Purpose

Chapter 15 is the second chapter in a three-chapter sequence that concentrates on short-run fluctuations in the economy around its long-run trend. In Chapter 14, we introduced the model of aggregate supply and aggregate demand. In Chapter 15, we see how the government's monetary and fiscal policies affect aggregate demand. In Chapter 16, we will see some of the tradeoffs between short-run and long-run objectives when we address the relationship between inflation and unemployment.

The purpose of Chapter 15 is to address the short-run effects of monetary and fiscal policies. In Chapter 14, we found that when aggregate demand or short-run aggregate supply shifts, it causes fluctuations in output. As a result, policymakers sometimes try to offset these shifts by shifting aggregate demand with monetary and fiscal policy. Chapter 15 addresses the theory behind these policies and some of the shortcomings of stabilization policy.

B. Helpful Hints

1. *Activist stabilization policy has many descriptive names.* Activist stabilization policy is the use of discretionary monetary and fiscal policies to manage aggregate demand in such a way as to minimize fluctuations in output and to maintain output at the long-run natural level. As such, activist stabilization policy is sometimes called *discretionary policy* to distinguish it from automatic stabilizers. It is also called *aggregate-demand management* because monetary and fiscal policies are used to adjust or manage total spending in the economy. Finally, since policy-makers attempt to counter the business cycle by reducing aggregate demand when it is too high and by increasing aggregate demand when it is too low, stabilization policy is sometimes referred to as *countercyclical policy.*

2. *Activist stabilization policy can be used to move output toward the long-run natural level from levels of output that are either above or below the natural level of output.* The examples of stabilization policy in the text assume the economy is in a recession — a period when output is below the long-run natural level. However, activist stabilization policy can be used to reduce aggregate demand and output in periods when output exceeds the long-run natural level. When output exceeds the natural level, we sometimes say that the economy is in a boom, an expansion, or that the economy is overheating. When the economy's output is above the natural level, the economy is said to be overheating because, left alone, the economy will adjust to a higher level of expected prices and wages, and output will fall to the natural level (short-run aggregate supply shifts left). Most economists believe that the Bank of Canada needs political independence to combat an overheating economy. This is

because the activist policy prescription for an overheating economy is a reduction in aggregate demand, which may encounter some political opposition. That is, "taking away the punch bowl just as the party gets going" is not likely to be politically popular.

3. *An important distinction between expansionary fiscal and monetary policy is the effect on interest rates in the short run.* An expansionary monetary policy (an increase in the money supply) lowers interest rates, which stimulates investment spending and shifts aggregate demand to the right. An expansionary fiscal policy (higher government spending or lower taxes) raises interest rates, which "crowds out" investment spending and partially reverses the initial increase in aggregate demand.

4. *In the long run in an open economy, Canada's interest rate must equal the world interest rate.* Under a flexible exchange rate, expansionary monetary policy causes the real exchange rate to depreciate, further stimulating aggregate demand. The rise in output and income increases money demand enough to lift Canada's interest rate up to the world interest rate. Expansionary fiscal policy causes the real exchange rate to appreciate, which depresses aggregate demand. The fall in output and income decreases money demand enough to drop Canada's interest rate down to the world interest rate.

5. *Under a fixed exchange rate, monetary policy is ineffective.* The Bank of Canada's responsibility to fix the external value of the Canadian dollar forces it to intervene in the foreign exchange market, which means that it loses control of the money supply. Fiscal policy is only effective under a fixed exchange rate; it has no crowding-out effects on investment or net exports, and thus has a lasting effect on aggregate demand.

II. Self-Testing Challenges

A. True/False Questions

_____1.   An increase in the interest rate increases the quantity demanded of money because it increases the rate of return on money.

_____2.   When money demand is drawn on a graph with the interest rate on the vertical axis and the quantity of money on the horizontal axis, an increase in the price level shifts money demand to the right.

_____3.   Keynes's theory of liquidity preference suggests that the interest rate is determined by the supply and demand for money.

_____4.   The interest rate effect suggests that the aggregate-demand curve slopes downward because an increase in the price level shifts money demand to the right, increases the interest rate, and reduces investment and consumption.

_____5. An increase in the money supply shifts the money supply to the right, increases the interest rate, and decreases investment and consumption, which shifts the aggregate-demand curve to the left.

_____6. Suppose investors and consumers become pessimistic about the future and cut back on expenditures. If the Bank of Canada engages in activist stabilization policy, the policy response should be to decrease the money supply.

_____7. The Bank of Canada cannot choose the size of the money supply and the external value of the Canadian dollar.

_____8. Because of the multiplier effect, an increase in government spending of $4 billion will shift the aggregate-demand curve to the right by more than $4 billion (assuming there is no crowding out).

_____9. If the MPC (marginal propensity to consume) is 0.80, then the value of the closed economy multiplier is 8.

_____10. Crowding out occurs in a closed economy when an increase in government spending increases incomes, shifts money demand to the right, raises the interest rate, and reduces private investment.

_____11. Suppose the government increases its expenditure in a closed economy by $2 billion. If the crowding-out effect exceeds the multiplier effect, then the aggregate-demand curve shifts to the right by more than $2 billion.

_____12. Suppose investors and consumers become pessimistic about the future and cut back on expenditures. If fiscal policymakers engage in activist stabilization policy, the policy response should be to decrease government spending and increase taxes.

_____13. Many economists prefer automatic stabilizers because they affect the economy with a shorter lag than activist stabilization policies.

_____14. In the short run, the interest rate is determined by money demand and money supply in a closed economy, but not in an open economy.

_____15. Employment Insurance benefits are an example of an automatic stabilizer because when incomes fall, Employment Insurance benefits rise.

B. Multiple-Choice Questions

1. Keynes's liquidity preference theory of the interest rate suggests that the interest rate is determined by
    a. the supply and demand for loanable funds.
    b. the supply and demand for money.
    c. the supply and demand for labour.
    d. aggregate supply and aggregate demand.

2. When money demand is expressed in a graph with the interest rate on the vertical axis and the quantity of money on the horizontal axis, an increase in the interest rate
   a. increases the quantity demanded of money.
   b. increases the demand for money.
   c. decreases the quantity demanded of money.
   d. decreases the demand for money.
   e. causes none of the above.

3. When the supply and demand for money are expressed in a graph with the interest rate on the vertical axis and the quantity of money on the horizontal axis, an increase in the price level
   a. shifts money demand to the right and increases the interest rate.
   b. shifts money demand to the left and increases the interest rate.
   c. shifts money demand to the right and decreases the interest rate.
   d. shifts money demand to the left and decreases the interest rate.
   e. causes none of the above.

4. In a closed economy, the most important reason for the downward slope of the aggregate-demand curve is
   a. the real exchange-rate effect.
   b. the wealth effect.
   c. the fiscal effect.
   d. the interest-rate effect.
   e. none of the above.

5. In the market for real output, the initial effect of an increase in the money supply is to
   a. shift aggregate demand to the right.
   b. shift aggregate demand to the left.
   c. shift aggregate supply to the right.
   d. shift aggregate supply to the left.

6. The short-run effect of an increase in the money supply in an open economy is to
   a. increase the exchange rate.
   b. decrease the price level.
   c. increase the interest rate.
   d. decrease the interest rate.

7. The long-run effect of an increase in the money supply in an open economy is
   a. greater under a flexible exchange rate.
   b. smaller than in a closed economy.
   c. greater under a fixed exchange rate.
   d. the same as in a closed economy.

8. Suppose a wave of investor and consumer pessimism causes a reduction in spending. If the Bank of Canada chooses to engage in activist stabilization policy, it should
   a. increase government spending and decrease taxes.
   b. decrease government spending and increase taxes.
   c. increase the money supply and decrease interest rates.
   d. decrease the money supply and increase interest rates.

9. A decrease in government spending shifts
   a. aggregate supply to the right.
   b. aggregate supply to the left.
   c. aggregate demand to the right.
   d. aggregate demand to the left.

10. If the marginal propensity to consume (MPC) is 0.75, and the marginal propensity to import (MPI) is 0.25, the value of the multiplier is
    a. 0.75.
    b. 2.
    c. 5.25.
    d. 7.5.
    e. none of the above.

11. An increase in the marginal propensity to consume (MPC)
    a. raises the value of the multiplier.
    b. lowers the value of the multiplier.
    c. has no impact on the value of the multiplier.
    d. rarely occurs because the MPC is set by federal law.

12. Suppose a wave of investor and consumer optimism has increased spending so that the current level of output exceeds the long-run natural level. If policymakers choose to engage in activist stabilization policy, they should
    a. decrease taxes, which shifts aggregate demand to the right.
    b. decrease taxes, which shifts aggregate demand to the left.
    c. decrease government spending, which shifts aggregate demand to the right.
    d. decrease government spending, which shifts aggregate demand to the left.

13. When an increase in government spending in the short run raises incomes, shifts money demand to the right, raises the interest rate, and lowers investment, we have seen a demonstration of
    a. the multiplier effect.
    b. the investment accelerator.
    c. the crowding-out effect.
    d. supply-side economics.
    e. none of the above.

14. Which of the following statements regarding taxes is correct?
    a. Most economists believe that, in the short run, the greatest impact of a change in taxes is on aggregate supply, not aggregate demand.
    b. A change in taxes has a greater effect on aggregate demand under a fixed exchange rate than a flexible exchange rate.
    c. An increase in taxes shifts the aggregate-demand curve to the right.
    d. A decrease in taxes shifts the aggregate-supply curve to the left.

15. Suppose the government increases expenditures by $6 billion. If the multiplier effect exceeds the crowding-out effect, then
    a. the aggregate-supply curve shifts to the right by more than $6 billion.
    b. the aggregate-supply curve shifts to the left by more than $6 billion.
    c. the aggregate-demand curve shifts to the right by more than $6 billion.
    d. the aggregate-demand curve shifts to the left by more than $6 billion.

16. When an increase in government spending increases the income of some people, and those people spend some of that increase in income on additional consumer goods, we have seen a demonstration of
    a. the multiplier effect.
    b. the investment accelerator.
    c. the crowding-out effect.
    d. supply-side economics.
    e. none of the above.

17. When an increase in government spending causes firms to purchase additional plant and equipment, we have seen a demonstration of
    a. the multiplier effect.
    b. the investment accelerator.
    c. the crowding-out effect.
    d. supply-side economics.
    e. none of the above.

18. Which of the following is an automatic stabilizer?
    a. military spending
    b. spending on public schools
    c. Employment Insurance benefits
    d. spending on civil service salaries
    e. All are automatic stabilizers.

19. Which of the following statements about stabilization policy is true?
    a. In the short run, a decision by the Bank of Canada to increase the money supply is essentially the same as a decision to increase the interest rate.
    b. Parliament has no role in the use of fiscal policy.
    c. Long lags enhance the ability of policymakers to "fine-tune" the economy.
    d. Many economists prefer automatic stabilizers because they affect the economy with a shorter lag than activist stabilization policy.
    e. All of the above are true.

20. Which of the following statements is correct?
    a. A flexible exchange rate eliminates the crowding-out effect on investment and net exports of an expansionary fiscal policy.
    b. Fiscal policy has no lasting impact on aggregate demand under a flexible exchange rate.
    c. The Coyne Affair illustrated the conflict between the federal and provincial governments regarding the coordinated use of fiscal policy.
    d. Keynes' book, *The General Theory of Employment, Interest, and Money*, emphasized the key role of aggregate supply in explaining short-run economic fluctuations.

C. Short-Answer Questions

1. Why is the money-supply curve vertical when it is drawn on a graph with the interest rate on the vertical axis and the quantity of money on the horizontal axis? _____
   _____
   _____
   _____

2. Why does the money-demand curve slope negatively when it is drawn on a graph with the interest rate on the vertical axis and the quantity of money on the horizontal axis? _____
   _____
   _____
   _____

3. Why does an increase in the price level reduce the quantity demanded of real output? (Use the interest rate effect to explain the slope of the aggregate-demand curve.) _____
   _____
   _____
   _____

4. Explain how an increase in the money supply shifts the aggregate-demand curve in the short run. _____
   _____
   _____
   _____

5. Explain the intuition of the multiplier effect resulting from an increase in government spending in a closed economy. Why should a bigger MPC make the multiplier effect larger? _____
   _____
   _____
   _____
   _____

6. Explain how an increase in government spending may lead to crowding out in an open economy. _____

_____

_____

_____

7. Suppose the government spends $2 billion dollars on a public works program that is intended to stimulate aggregate demand in a closed economy. If the crowding-out effect exceeds the multiplier effect, will the aggregate-demand curve shift to the right by more or less than $2 billion? Why? _____

_____

_____

8. How does a cut in taxes affect aggregate supply? _____

_____

9. Which is likely to have a greater impact on aggregate demand: A decrease in taxes with a flexible or fixed exchange rate? Why? _____

_____

_____

10. Explain why taxes and government spending may act as automatic stabilizers. What would a strict balanced-budget rule cause policymakers to do during a recession? Would this make the recession more or less severe? _____

_____

_____

_____

D. Practice Problems

1. If the Bank of Canada was to engage in activist stabilization policy, in which direction should it move the money supply in response to the following events?

   a. A wave of optimism boosts business investment and household consumption.

   _____

   b. OPEC raises the price of crude oil. _____

   c. Foreigners reduce their demand for Canadian lumber. _____

2. If the minister of finance was to use fiscal policy to actively stabilize the economy, in which direction should government spending and taxes change?

   a. A wave of pessimism reduces business investment and household consumption.

   _____

   _____

b. Foreigners increase their demand for Canadian-produced telecommunications equipment. _____

_____

c. The world price of crude oil falls. _____

3. Suppose the economy is in a recession. Policymakers estimate that aggregate demand is $10 billion short of the amount necessary to generate the long-run natural level of output. That is, if aggregate demand were shifted to the right by $10 billion, the economy would be in long-run equilibrium.

a. If the federal government chooses to use fiscal policy to stabilize the economy, by how much should they increase government spending if the marginal propensity to consume (MPC) is 0.75, the economy is closed, and there is no crowding out?_____

_____

_____

b. If the federal government chooses to use fiscal policy to stabilize the economy, by how much should they increase government spending if the marginal propensity to consume (MPC) is 0.75, the marginal propensity to import (MPI) in the open economy is 0.25, and there is no crowding out? _____

_____

_____

c. If there is crowding out of investment spending in a closed economy, will the government need to spend more or less than the amount you found in (a) above? Why? _____

_____

_____

_____

d. If investment spending by firms in a closed economy is very sensitive to changes in the interest rate, is crowding out more of a problem or less of a problem? Why? _____

_____

_____

_____

e. If policymakers discover that the lag for fiscal policy in a closed economy is two years, should that make them more likely to employ fiscal policy as a stabilization tool or more likely to allow the economy to adjust on its own? Why? _____

_____

_____

_____

4. a. What does an increase in the money supply do to interest rates in an open economy in the short run? Explain. _____

_____

_____

_____

b. What does an increase in the money supply do to interest rates in an open economy in the long run? Explain. _____

_____

_____

_____

c. Are these results inconsistent? Explain. _____

_____

_____

_____

E. Advanced Critical Thinking

You are watching a nightly network news broadcast. The business correspondent reports that the Bank of Canada raised interest rates by a quarter of a percent today to head off future inflation. The report then moves to interviews with prominent politicians. The response of the leader of the official opposition is negative. She says, "The Consumer Price Index has not increased, yet the Bank of Canada is restricting growth in the economy, supposedly to fight inflation. My constituents will want to know why they are going to have to pay more when they get a loan, and I don't have a good answer. I think this is an outrage and I think Parliament should have hearings on the Bank of Canada's policy-making powers."

1. What interest rate did the Bank of Canada raise? _____

2. State the Bank of Canada's policy in terms of the money supply. _____

_____

3. Why might the Bank of Canada raise interest rates before the CPI starts to rise? _____

_____

_____

_____

4. Use the opposition politician's statement to explain why most economists believe that the Bank of Canada needs to be independent of politics. _____

_____

_____

_____

III. Solutions

A. True/False Questions

1. F; an increase in the interest rate decreases the quantity demanded of money because it raises the opportunity cost of holding money.
2. T
3. T
4. T
5. F; an increase in the money supply decreases the interest rate, and increases investment and consumption, which shifts aggregate demand to the right.
6. F; the Bank of Canada should increase the money supply.
7. T
8. T
9. F; the value of the multiplier is 5.
10. T
11. F; the aggregate-demand curve shifts to the right by less than $2 billion.
12. F; policymakers should increase government spending and decrease taxes.
13. T
14. F; in the short run, the interest rate is determined by money demand and money supply in both open and closed economies.
15. T

B. Multiple-Choice Questions

1. b	6. d	11. a	16. a
2. c	7. a	12. d	17. b
3. a	8. c	13. c	18. c
4. d	9. d	14. b	19. d
5. a	10. b	15. c	20. b

C. Short-Answer Questions

1. Because the quantity of money is fixed at whatever value the Bank of Canada chooses and this quantity is not dependent on the interest rate.

2. The interest rate is the opportunity cost of money since money earns no rate of return. Thus, an increase in the interest rate causes people to economize on cash balances and hold more wealth in interest-bearing bonds.

3. An increase in the price level shifts money demand to the right, increases the interest rate, and decreases investment and consumption expenditures.

4. The money-supply curve shifts right, the interest rate decreases, and investment and consumption increase at each price level, which is a rightward shift in the aggregate-demand curve.

5. When the government purchases goods and services, it causes an increase in the incomes of the sellers. They spend some proportion of their new higher income on goods and services, raising other's incomes, and so on. The higher the MPC, the greater the proportion of new income spent in each round.

6. An increase in government spending raises incomes, shifts money demand right, raises the interest rate, and crowds out investment. With a flexible exchange rate, the Canadian dollar appreciates, which crowds out net exports.

7. By less than $2 billion because the crowding-out effect, which reduces the shift in aggregate demand, more than offsets the multiplier effect, which amplifies the shift.

8. It causes an increase in aggregate supply by increasing the incentive to work.

9. A decrease in taxes with a fixed exchange rate, because fiscal policy has no crowding-out effect on investment or net exports.

10. Income tax collections fall during recession and government spending on welfare and Employment Insurance benefits rises. Both of these stimulate aggregate demand. It would cause the government to raise other taxes and lower other spending. More severe.

D. Practice Problems

1. a. Decrease the money supply

   b. Increase the money supply

   c. Increase the money supply

2. a. Increase spending, decrease taxes

   b. Decrease spending, increase taxes

   c. Decrease spending, increase taxes

3. a. Multiplier $= 1/(1 - 0.75) = 4$. $10/4 = $2.5 billion.

   b. Multiplier $= 1/(1 - 0.75 + 0.25) = 2$. $10/2 = $5 billion.

   c. More, because as the government spends more, firms spend less on plant and equipment so aggregate demand won't increase by as much as the multiplier suggests.

   d. More of a problem. Government spending raises interest rates. The more sensitive investment is to the interest rate, the more it is reduced or crowded out by government spending.

e. More likely to allow the economy to adjust on its own because if the economy adjusts on its own before the impact of the fiscal policy is felt, the fiscal policy will be destabilizing.

4. a. It lowers interest rates. An increase in the money supply requires a decrease in interest rates to induce people to hold the additional money.

   b. It has no effect because, in the long run, Canada's interest rate must equal the world interest rate.

   c. No. In the short run, interest rates adjust to balance the supply and demand for money. In the long run, Canada's interest rate equals the world interest rate, and net foreign investment adjusts to balance the supply and demand for loanable funds.

E. Advanced Critical Thinking

1. The bank rate.

2. They decreased the money supply (or lowered its growth rate).

3. Because monetary policy acts on the economy with a lag. If the Bank of Canada waits until inflation has arrived, the effect of its policy will arrive too late. Thus, the Bank of Canada responds to its forecast of inflation.

4. Politicians must be responsive to the short-term needs of voters. Monetary policy must take a long-term view and make politically painful decisions when the economy is overheating (when output is above the long-run natural level).

Chapter 16: The Short-Run Tradeoff between
Inflation and Unemployment

I. Chapter Overview

A. Context and Purpose

Chapter 16 is the final chapter in a three-chapter sequence on the economy's short-run fluctuations around its long-run trend. Chapter 14 introduced aggregate supply and aggregate demand. Chapter 15 developed how monetary and fiscal policy affect aggregate demand. Both Chapter 14 and 15 addressed relationships between the price level and output. Chapter 16 will concentrate on a similar relationship between inflation and unemployment.

The purpose of Chapter 16 is to trace the history of economists' thinking about the relationship between inflation and unemployment. You will see why there is a temporary tradeoff between inflation and unemployment, and why there is no permanent tradeoff. This result is an extension of the events in the model of aggregate supply and aggregate demand where a change in the price level induced by a change in aggregate demand temporarily alters output but has no permanent impact on output.

B. Helpful Hints

1. *Short-run and long-run Phillips curves are almost a mirror image of short-run and long-run aggregate-supply curves.* Look at Figures 16-2 and 16-4 of the text. Notice the aggregate-supply curves in panel (a). Compare them to the Phillips curves in panel (b). They appear to be mirror images of each other. The long-run aggregate-supply curve is vertical because, in the long run, an increase in the price level is met by a proportionate increase in all prices and incomes so there is no incentive to alter production. Since an increase in prices has no effect on output in the long run, it has no effect on unemployment, and the long-run Phillips curve is vertical in panel (b). In the short-run with price expectations fixed, an increase in the price level provides an incentive for firms to increase production, which causes the short-run aggregate-supply curve to be positively sloped in panel (a). When output rises, unemployment tends to fall, so the short-run Phillips curve is negatively sloped in panel (b). In summary, since both graphs employ some measure of prices on the vertical axis, and since each graph uses real measures of economic activity that are negatively correlated on their respective horizontal axes (an increase in output is associated with a decrease in unemployment) then aggregate-supply curves and Phillips curves should "mirror" each other.

2. *To understand the short-run Phillips curve, review the short-run aggregate-supply curve.* To gain confidence deriving and shifting short-run Phillips curves, review the sources to the positive slope of the short-run aggregate-supply curve in Chapter 14. There you will be reminded that there are a number of reasons why a short-run aggregate-supply curve slopes positively — misperceptions about relative price,

sticky wages, and sticky prices. Since short-run aggregate-supply curves and Phillips curves are mirror images of each other, the very same reasons that produce a positive slope in aggregate supply produce a negative slope in the Phillips curve. Also, recall that all three theories of the short-run aggregate-supply curve are based on the assumption of fixed price expectations. When expected inflation rises, the short-run aggregate-supply curve shifts left. Correspondingly, since the short-run aggregate-supply curve and the Phillips curve are mirror images, a rise in expected inflation shifts the Phillips curve to the right.

3. *Estimates of the natural rate of unemployment vary widely causing policymakers to disagree on the appropriate monetary and fiscal policies.* When looking at a Phillips curve graph or the model of aggregate supply and aggregate demand, it appears as if policymakers should always know whether to expand or contract aggregate demand or whether to leave aggregate demand alone. This is because we can see whether the economy is operating above or below the long-run natural rate that we have chosen on the graph. In reality, however, the natural rate of unemployment is very difficult to measure and policymakers are uncertain whether the economy is actually operating above or below the natural rate. For example, if the economy is currently operating at 8% unemployment, the economy is operating below capacity if the natural rate of unemployment is 7%, at capacity if the natural rate is 8%, and above capacity if the natural rate is 9%. Each situation might suggest a different stabilization policy, even though the actual rate of unemployment is unchanged at 8%.

II. Self-Testing Challenges

A. True/False Questions

_____1. The Phillips curve illustrates the positive relationship between inflation and unemployment.

_____2. If inflation is 4% and unemployment is 6%, the misery index is 2%.

_____3. In the short run, an increase in aggregate demand increases the price level and output, and decreases unemployment.

_____4. When unemployment is below the natural rate, the labour market is unusually tight putting pressure on wages and prices to rise.

_____5. An increase in expected inflation shifts the Phillips curve to the right and makes the inflation unemployment tradeoff less favourable.

_____6. An increase in the money supply increases inflation and permanently decreases unemployment.

_____7. In the long run, the unemployment rate is independent of inflation and the Phillips curve is vertical at the natural rate of unemployment.

_____8. When actual inflation exceeds expected inflation, unemployment exceeds the natural rate.

_____9.   The natural-rate hypothesis suggests that, in the long run, unemployment returns to its natural rate, regardless of inflation.

_____10.   An adverse supply shock, such as an increase in the price of imported oil, shifts the Phillips curve to the right and makes the inflation unemployment tradeoff less favourable.

_____11.   A decrease in Employment Insurance benefits reduces the natural rate of unemployment and shifts the long-run Phillips curve to the right.

_____12.   An increase in aggregate demand temporarily reduces unemployment, but after people raise their expectations of inflation, unemployment returns to the natural rate.

_____13.   A sudden monetary contraction moves the economy up a short-run Phillips curve, reducing unemployment and increasing inflation.

_____14.   If people have rational expectations, an announced monetary contraction by the Bank of Canada that is credible could reduce inflation with little or no increase in unemployment.

_____15.   If the sacrifice ratio is 4, a reduction of inflation from 9% to 5% requires a reduction in output of 8%.

B. Multiple-Choice Questions

1. The misery index, which some commentators suggest measures the health of the economy, is
    a.   the sum of the growth rate of output and the inflation rate.
    b.   the sum of the unemployment rate and the inflation rate.
    c.   the sum of the unemployment rate and the bank rate.
    d.   the sum of the natural rate of unemployment and the actual rate of unemployment.

2. The original Phillips curve illustrates
    a.   the tradeoff between inflation and unemployment.
    b.   the positive relationship between inflation and unemployment.
    c.   the tradeoff between output and unemployment.
    d.   the positive relationship between output and unemployment.

3. The Phillips curve is an extension of the model of aggregate supply and aggregate demand because, in the short run, an increase in aggregate demand increases the price level and
    a.   decreases growth.
    b.   decreases inflation.
    c.   increases unemployment.
    d.   decreases unemployment.

4. Along a short-run Phillips curve,
   a. a higher rate of growth in output is associated with a lower inflation rate.
   b. a higher rate of growth in output is associated with a higher unemployment rate.
   c. a higher rate of inflation is associated with a lower unemployment rate.
   d. a higher rate of inflation is associated with a higher unemployment rate.

5. If, in the long run, people adjust their price expectations so that all prices and incomes move proportionately to an increase in the price level, then the long-run Phillips curve
   a. is positively sloped.
   b. is negatively sloped.
   c. is vertical.
   d. has a slope that is determined by how fast people adjust their price expectations.

6. According to the Phillips curve, in the short run, if policymakers choose an expansionary fiscal or monetary policy to lower the rate of unemployment,
   a. the economy will experience a decrease in inflation.
   b. the economy will experience an increase in inflation.
   c. inflation will be unaffected if price expectations are unchanging.
   d. none of the above.

7. An increase in expected inflation
   a. shifts the short-run Phillips curve to the right and the unemployment inflation tradeoff is less favourable.
   b. shifts the short-run Phillips curve to the left and the unemployment inflation tradeoff is more favourable.
   c. shifts the short-run Phillips curve to the right and the unemployment inflation tradeoff is more favourable.
   d. shifts the short-run Phillips curve to the left and the unemployment inflation tradeoff is less favourable.

8. Which of the following would shift the long-run Phillips curve to the right?
   a. an increase in the price of foreign oil
   b. an increase in expected inflation
   c. an increase in aggregate demand
   d. an increase in the minimum wage

9. If actual inflation exceeds expected inflation,
   a. unemployment is greater than the natural rate of unemployment.
   b. unemployment is less than the natural rate of unemployment.
   c. unemployment is equal to the natural rate of unemployment.
   d. in the future, people will reduce their expectations of inflation.

10. A decrease in the price of foreign oil
    a. shifts the short-run Phillips curve to the right and the unemployment inflation tradeoff is more favourable.

b. shifts the short-run Phillips curve to the right and the unemployment inflation tradeoff is less favourable.

c. shifts the short-run Phillips curve to the left and the unemployment inflation tradeoff is more favourable.

d. shifts the short-run Phillips curve to the left and the unemployment inflation tradeoff is less favourable.

11. The natural-rate hypothesis argues that
a. unemployment is always above the natural rate.
b. unemployment is always below the natural rate.
c. unemployment is always equal to the natural rate.
d. in the long run, the unemployment rate returns to the natural rate, regardless of inflation.

Use the following graph for questions 12-17.

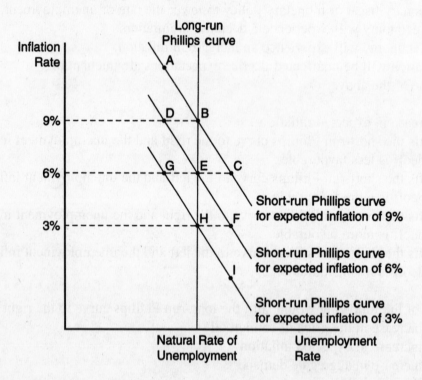

12. If people in the economy expect inflation to be 3% and inflation is 3%, the economy is operating at point
a. A.
b. B.
c. C.
d. D.
e. E.
f. F.
g. G.
h. H.
i. I.

13. If people in the economy expect inflation to be 6% but inflation turns out to be 3%, the economy is operating at point
    a. A.
    b. B.
    c. C.
    d. D.
    e. E.
    f. F.
    g. G.
    h. H.
    i. I.

14. Suppose the economy is in long-run equilibrium at point E. A sudden increase in government spending should move the economy in the direction of point
    a. A.
    b. B.
    c. C.
    d. D.
    e. E.
    f. F.
    g. G.
    h. H.
    i. I.

15. Suppose the economy is operating at point D. As people revise their price expectations,
    a. the short-run Phillips curve will shift in the direction of the short-run Phillips curve associated with an expectation of 3% inflation.
    b. the short-run Phillips curve will shift in the direction of the short-run Phillips curve associated with an expectation of 6% inflation.
    c. the short-run Phillips curve will shift in the direction of the short-run Phillips curve associated with an expectation of 9% inflation.
    d. the long-run Phillips curve will shift to the left.

16. Suppose the economy is operating in long-run equilibrium at point E. An unexpected monetary contraction will move the economy in the direction of point
    a. A.
    b. B.
    c. C.
    d. D.
    e. E.
    f. F.
    g. G.
    h. H.
    i. I.

17. Suppose the economy is operating in long-run equilibrium at point E. In the long run, a monetary contraction will move the economy in the direction of point
    a. A.
    b. B.
    c. C.
    d. D.
    e. E.
    f. F.
    g. G.
    h. H.
    i. I.

18. If people have rational expectations, a monetary policy contraction that is announced and is credible could
    a. reduce inflation but it would increase unemployment by an unusually large amount.
    b. reduce inflation with little or no increase in unemployment.
    c. increase inflation but it would decrease unemployment by an unusually large amount.
    d. increase inflation with little or no decrease in unemployment.

19. If the sacrifice ratio is 5, a reduction in inflation from 7% to 3% would require
    a. a reduction in output of 5%.
    b. a reduction in output of 15%.
    c. a reduction in output of 20%.
    d. a reduction in output of 35%.

20. If the Bank of Canada were to continuously use expansionary monetary policy in an attempt to hold unemployment below the natural rate, the long-run result would be
    a. an increase in the level of output.
    b. a decrease in the unemployment rate.
    c. an increase in the rate of inflation.
    d. all of the above.

C. Short-Answer Questions

1. If unemployment is 6% and inflation is 5%, what is the value of the so-called misery index? _____

    _____

2. Use the model of aggregate demand and aggregate supply to describe why the short-run Phillips curve is negatively sloped. _____

    _____

    _____

    _____

3. Use the model of aggregate demand and aggregate supply to describe why the long-run Phillips curve is vertical. _____

    _____

    _____

    _____

4. Is the short-run Phillips curve actually a menu of inflation and unemployment combinations permanently available to the policymaker? Why? _____

    _____

    _____

    _____

    _____

5. What is the natural-rate hypothesis? _____

    _____

    _____

6. If actual inflation exceeds expected inflation, is the unemployment rate above or below the natural rate? Why? _____

    _____

    _____

7. Which way does the short-run Phillips curve shift when there is an adverse aggregate-supply shock, such as, an increase in the price of imported oil? Why? _____

    _____

    _____

8. Referring to question 7 above, are the tradeoffs between unemployment and inflation that the economy now faces more favourable or less favourable than before the adverse aggregate-supply shock? Explain. _____

    _____

    _____

    _____

9. Referring to question 8 above, if the Bank of Canada accommodates the adverse aggregate-supply shock, what have they revealed about the weights they attach to the goals of low inflation and low unemployment? _____

    _____

10. If the sacrifice ratio is 2, how much will output be reduced in order for inflation to be reduced by 4 percentage points? If people have rational expectations, is the sacrifice ratio likely to be larger or smaller than 2? Why? _____

    _____

    _____

D. Practice Problems

1. Describe the initial effect of the following events on the short-run or long-run
    Phillips curve. That is, describe the movements along a given curve or the direction
    of the shift in the curve.

    a. An increase in expected inflation. _____
        _____

    b. An increase in the price of imported oil. _____
        _____

    c. An increase in the money supply. _____
        _____

    d. A decrease in government spending. _____
        _____

    e. A decrease in the minimum wage that lowers the natural rate of unemployment.
        _____
        _____

2. Use the Phillips curves in the following graph to answer the following questions.

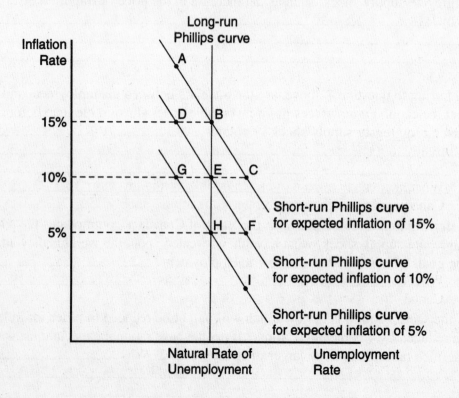

a. At what point is the economy located if people expect 10% inflation and inflation is actually 10%? _____

b. Referring to (a) above, is unemployment above, below, or equal to the natural rate? _____

c. At what point is the economy located if people expect 10% inflation and the actual rate of inflation is 15%? _____

_____

d. Suppose the economy is operating at point D. Over time, in which direction will people revise their expectations of inflation — up or down? _____

_____

e. Suppose the economy is operating at point D. As people revise their expectations of inflation, in which direction will the short-run Phillips curve shift — right or left? _____

f. Suppose the economy is operating at point E. In the short run, a sudden decrease in aggregate demand will move the economy toward which point? _____

_____

g. Suppose the economy is operating at point E. In the long run, a decrease in government spending will tend to move the economy toward which point? _____

_____

h. Suppose people expect 5% inflation. If inflation actually ends up being 10%, in which direction will unemployment move — above or below the natural rate?

_____

3. Use a Phillips curve graph to answer the following questions. Assume the economy is initially in long-run equilibrium.

a. What happens to unemployment and inflation in the short run if the Bank of Canada increases the growth rate of the money supply? _____

_____

_____

b. What happens to unemployment and inflation in the long run if the Bank of Canada increases the growth rate of the money supply? _____

_____

_____

c. Can printing money keep unemployment below the natural rate? Explain. _____

_____

_____

d. What is the end result of a central bank repeatedly attempting to hold unemployment below the natural rate with expansionary monetary policy? Explain. _____

_____

_____

4. Suppose the economy is operating at the natural rate of unemployment with a high rate of inflation (point A in the following graph). Suppose the Bank of Canada announces a sudden monetary contraction to reduce inflation. Shown below are two possible paths the economy might take to adjust to the new lower rate of money growth. Choose the path that best depicts what might happen in each of the following cases and explain your reasoning.

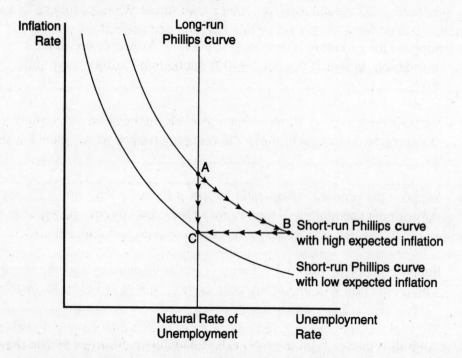

a. The Bank of Canada's announcement is not believed. _____

_____

_____

b. The Bank of Canada's announcement is believed and expectations of inflation are adjusted quickly. _____

_____

_____

c. The Bank of Canada's announcement is believed but all workers have long-term wage contracts that cannot be renegotiated. _____

_____

_____

d. Which of the above cases (a, b, or c) best describes what would happen if, in the past, the Bank of Canada had repeatedly announced that inflation is its number one priority, but it failed to actually engage in the threatened monetary contraction? Why? _____

_____

_____

E. Advanced Critical Thinking

A worldwide drought has reduced food production. Inflation has increased, unemployment has risen above the natural rate. Canadians are frustrated with their government. Your roommate says, "This economic mess has got to be somebody's fault. A year ago, both inflation and unemployment were lower. We need to vote in some new politicians that know how to get rid of this inflation and unemployment."

1. The stagflation present in the economy is the fault of whom? _____

_____

2. Are the current inflation and unemployment choices facing the economy better or worse than before the supply shock? What has happened to the short-run Phillips curve? _____

_____

3. If policymakers increase aggregate demand in response to the supply shock, in what direction will the economy move along the new short-run Phillips curve? What will happen to inflation and unemployment? _____

_____

_____

4. If policymakers decrease aggregate demand in response to the supply shock, in what direction will the economy move along the new short-run Phillips curve? What will happen to inflation and unemployment? _____

_____

_____

5. Is there a policy that can immediately reduce both inflation and unemployment? Explain. _____

_____

III. Solutions

A. True/False Questions

1. F; the Phillips curve illustrates the negative relationship between inflation and unemployment.
2. F; the misery index is 10%.

3. T
4. T
5. T
6. F; an increase in the money supply may temporarily decrease unemployment.
7. T
8. F; when actual inflation exceeds expected inflation, unemployment is below the natural rate.
9. T
10. T
11. F; it shifts the long-run Phillips curve to the left.
12. T
13. F; a sudden monetary contraction moves the economy down a short-run Phillips curve, increasing unemployment and reducing inflation.
14. T
15. F; output must be reduced by $4 \times 4\% = 16\%$.

B. Multiple-Choice Questions

1. b	6. b	11. d	16. f
2. a	7. a	12. h	17. h
3. d	8. d	13. f	18. b
4. c	9. b	14. d	19. c
5. c	10. c	15. c	20. c

C. Short-Answer Questions

1. 11%.

2. An increase in aggregate demand increases the price level and output along the short-run aggregate-supply curve, which reduces unemployment. Inflation has increased and unemployment has decreased.

3. An increase in aggregate demand increases the price level, but output remains at the natural level due to a vertical long-run aggregate-supply curve. Inflation has increased but unemployment remains at the natural rate.

4. No. When inflation increases above expected inflation, unemployment temporarily decreases. However, after people revise their price expectations upward, the Phillips curve shifts to the right.

5. Unemployment returns to the natural rate in the long run, regardless of inflation.

6. Below, because if prices are higher than expected more output is produced and more people are employed, reducing unemployment.

7. Aggregate supply shifts left showing lower production at each price. Thus, the Phillips curve shifts right showing more unemployment at each rate of inflation.

8. Less favourable. Now, at each level of unemployment, inflation is higher, or at each rate of inflation, unemployment is higher.

9. The Bank of Canada is more concerned with low unemployment.

10. 8%. Smaller because they will reduce their price expectations more quickly, shifting the Phillips curve to the left.

D. Practice Problems

1. a. Shifts short-run Phillips curve to the right.

   b. Shifts short-run Phillips curve to the right.

   c. Move up the short-run Phillips curve.

   d. Move down the short-run Phillips curve.

   e. Long-run Phillips curve shifts left.

2. a. E

   b. Equal to the natural rate.

   c. D

   d. Up.

   e. Right.

   f. F

   g. H

   h. Below the natural rate.

3. a. Inflation increases, unemployment decreases.

   b. Inflation increases, unemployment stays at the natural rate.

   c. No. Unemployment temporarily decreases, but as people grow to expect the higher inflation, unemployment returns to the natural rate.

   d. Continued attempts to move unemployment below the natural rate simply cause inflation.

4. a. Economy moves from A to B because people fail to reduce their price
        expectations and wage demands, so unemployment rises as inflation falls.

    b. Economy moves from A to C because people reduce their prices and wages
        proportionately.

    c. Economy moves from A to B because people are unable to actually reduce some
        of their wages and prices, so unemployment rises as inflation falls.

    d. Case (a), because people are rational to distrust a policymaker that has been
        untruthful before.

E. Advanced Critical Thinking

1. No one. It was an act of nature.

2. Worse because the short-run Phillips curve has shifted to the right.

3. The economy moves upward along the new short-run Phillips curve. Unemployment
    will be reduced but inflation will be increased.

4. The economy moves downward along the new short-run Phillips curve. Inflation
    will be reduced but unemployment will be increased.

5. No, the economy faces tradeoffs in the short run. A policy that reduces inflation
    increases unemployment. A policy that reduces unemployment increases inflation.

Chapter 17: Five Debates over Macroeconomic Policy

I. Chapter Overview

A. Context and Purpose

Chapter 17 is the final chapter in the text. It addresses five unresolved issues in macroeconomics, each of which is central to current political debates. The chapter can be studied all at once, or portions of the chapter can be studied in conjunction with prior chapters that deal with the related material.

The purpose of Chapter 17 is to provide both sides of five leading debates over macroeconomic policy. It employs information and tools you have accumulated in your study of this text. This chapter may help you take a position on the issues addressed or, at least, it may help you understand the reasoning of others who have taken a position.

B. Helpful Hints

1. *A policy that destabilizes the economy moves the economy away from the natural level of output.* Stabilization policy is the use of monetary and fiscal policy to help move the economy toward the natural level of output. However, if policy lags are long and unpredictable, the economy may have adjusted back to the natural level (from an aggregate-demand or aggregate-supply shock) before the impact of the stabilization policy is felt. In this case, the stabilization policy would then move the economy away from the long-run natural level and we would consider the policy to be destabilizing.

2. *A political business cycle tends to involve both a monetary expansion prior to an election and a monetary contraction after an election.* Political business cycles are discussed in the text with regard to the policymaker's behaviour prior to elections. That is, prior to an election, a monetary expansion could increase output and decrease unemployment, enhancing the probability of the incumbent party's re-election. Since this will tend to cause inflation after the election, however, this type of abuse of power usually involves a monetary contraction after the election to reduce inflationary pressures. Thus, the economy would tend to fluctuate between good economic performance prior to an election and poor economic performance after an election.

3. *Most economists support a cyclically balanced budget.* Federal government spending and tax collections depend on the level of output. For example, when output is above normal, Employment Insurance expenditures decrease and tax collections increase, moving the budget toward surplus. When output is below normal, Employment Insurance expenditures increase and tax collections decrease, moving the budget toward deficit. Inflexible rules requiring a continuously balanced budget would require the government to reduce spending or raise taxes during

recessions and raise government spending or cut taxes during economic booms, both of which would destabilize the economy further. Therefore, most economists suggest that the budget be balanced over the course of a business cycle, or what is termed a cyclically balanced budget, as opposed to a budget that is balanced each and every year.

II. Self-Testing Challenges

A. True/False Questions

_____1.   Monetary policy affects the economy with a lag but fiscal policy has no lag.

_____2.   Monetary policy may suffer from time inconsistency because policymakers have an incentive to engage in a policy that differs from their policy announcements.

_____3.   The political business cycle refers to a situation where corporate executives also hold political office.

_____4.   Opponents of an independent central bank argue that monetary policy is not an effective tool to influence voters.

_____5.   Supporters of a zero inflation target for monetary policy argue that the cost of reducing inflation is temporary while the benefits of reducing inflation are permanent.

_____6.   Those opposed to a zero inflation target for monetary policy argue that some of the costs of inflation can be eliminated by inflation-indexed taxes and bonds.

_____7.   Government debt tends to redistribute wealth from the current generation to future generations.

_____8.   Canada has only incurred federal government budget deficits during wars and recessions.

_____9.   Replacing the income tax with a consumption tax may increase saving, but it will tend to benefit the rich more than the poor.

_____10.   A reduction in taxes on interest income will increase saving if the substitution effect from the increase in after-tax interest outweighs the income effect.

B. Multiple-Choice Questions

1. Suppose that the economy is suffering from pessimism on the part of consumers and firms. Which of the following is an activist stabilization policy that "leans against the wind"?
    a. Policymakers should increase the money supply.
    b. Policymakers should increase taxes.
    c. Policymakers should decrease government spending.
    d. Policymakers should increase interest rates.
    e. None of the above.

2. Economists who argue that policymakers should not try to stabilize the economy make all of the following arguments except:
   a. Since stabilization policy affects the economy with a lag, well-intended policy could be destabilizing.
   b. Since forecasting shocks to the economy is difficult, well-intended policy could be destabilizing.
   c. Stabilization policy has no effect on the economy in the short run or the long run.
   d. The first rule of policymaking should be "do no harm."

3. Fluctuations in the economy caused by a policymaker's manipulation of the economy for the purpose of affecting electoral outcomes is known as
   a. the political business cycle.
   b. the time inconsistency of policy.
   c. the discretionary effect.
   d. the substitution effect.
   e. the income effect.

4. The discrepancy between policy announcements and policy actions is known as
   a. the political business cycle.
   b. the time inconsistency of policy.
   c. the discretionary effect.
   d. the substitution effect.
   e. the income effect.

5. Economists who argue that monetary policy should be made by an independent central bank make all of the following arguments except:
   a. It eliminates the political business cycle problem.
   b. It leads to a lower rate of inflation in the long run.
   c. It increases accountability for monetary policy choices.
   d. It eliminates the time inconsistency problem.

6. Which of the following is an example of an activist policy action that further destabilizes the economy?
   a. Investors become pessimistic and the Bank of Canada responds with a reduction in interest rates.
   b. Consumers become pessimistic and fiscal policymakers respond with a reduction in taxes.
   c. Investors become excessively optimistic and the Bank of Canada responds with a reduction in the money supply.
   d. Consumers become pessimistic and fiscal policymakers respond with a reduction in government spending.

7. Economists who support a zero inflation target for monetary policy make all of the following arguments except:
   a. Inflation imposes permanent costs on the economy such as shoeleather costs and menu costs.

b. When there is zero inflation, people's standard of living is no longer eroded by their incomes failing to increase with inflation.

c. The cost of reducing inflation to zero is temporary while the benefits are permanent.

d. The cost of reducing inflation to zero could be reduced if a zero inflation policy were credible.

8. The government debt tends to
   a. redistribute wealth from future generations to the current generation.
   b. redistribute wealth from the current generation to future generations.
   c. have no redistributive effects.
   d. none of the above.

9. Which of the following is not true with regard to government budget deficits?
   a. Budget deficits place the burden of current spending on future taxpayers.
   b. Budget deficits reduce national saving.
   c. Budget deficits should be scrutinized because they are the only way to transfer income across generations of taxpayers.
   d. Budget deficits reduce capital investment, future productivity and, therefore, future incomes.

10. Economists who argue that the central bank should not aim for zero inflation realize that
    a. the social costs of disinflation are smaller than the economic costs of disinflation.
    b. the cost of reducing inflation is concentrated on those workers who lose their jobs.
    c. those who lose their jobs often have the most skills and experience.
    d. all of the above.

11. Economists who argue that the government need not reduce the government debt make all of the following arguments except:
    a. The government debt per person is relatively small compared to a person's lifetime earnings.
    b. If parents save more and leave a larger bequest, there is no intergenerational redistribution of wealth from budget deficits.
    c. Budget deficits will not become an increasing burden as long as the debt does not grow more quickly than a nation's nominal income.
    d. Budget deficits increase future growth because they transfer wealth from the present generation to future generations.

12. Which of the following changes to tax laws would encourage more saving but also increase the tax burden on low-income people?
    a. Reduce taxes on the return to saving.
    b. Increase the maximum amount that households can contribute to an RRSP.
    c. Increase the GST from 7% to 9%, while lowering personal income tax rates.
    d. Replace the income tax with a consumption tax.
    e. All of the above.

13. A reduction in taxes that increases the after-tax return to saving will increase the quantity of saving in the economy if
    a. the substitution effect from the increase in after-tax return to saving exceeds the income effect.
    b. the income effect from the increase in after-tax return to saving exceeds the substitution effect.
    c. the income effect from the increase in after-tax return to saving equals the substitution effect.
    d. the policy is time inconsistent.

14. Tax reform that encourages saving tends to
    a. shift the tax burden toward high-income people away from low-income people.
    b. shift the tax burden toward low-income people away from high-income people.
    c. reduce the rate of growth of output.
    d. reduce the budget deficit.

15. If monetary policy is time inconsistent
    a. the long-run Phillips curve shifts to the right.
    b. the long-run Phillips curve shifts to the left.
    c. the short-run Phillips curve shifts upward.
    d. the short-run Phillips curve shifts downward.

C. Short-Answer Questions

1. Why would an improvement in our ability to forecast shocks to the macroeconomy improve our use of activist stabilization policy? _____
   _____
   _____

2. What two reasons are given in support of an independent central bank? _____
   _____
   _____

3. Why are the costs of inflation permanent but the costs of reducing inflation temporary? _____
   _____
   _____
   _____

4. What could the federal government do to reduce some of the costs of continuous inflation? _____
   _____
   _____

5. In what two ways does the government debt harm future generations? _____
   _____
   _____

6. Does a balanced federal government budget guarantee the elimination of all redistributions of wealth across generations? Explain. _____

_____

_____

_____

7. For an increase in the after-tax return to saving to cause an increase in saving, which effect must outweigh the other — the substitution effect or the income effect? Why? _____

_____

_____

_____

8. Why will reforming our tax laws to encourage saving tend to increase the tax burden on the poor? _____

_____

_____

_____

D. Practice Problems

1. Suppose a wave of pessimism engulfs consumers and firms causing them to reduce their expenditures.

a. Demonstrate this event with the model of aggregate demand and aggregate supply assuming that the economy was originally in long-run equilibrium.

b. What is the appropriate activist policy response for monetary and fiscal policy? In which direction would the activist policy shift aggregate demand? _____
_____
_____

c. Suppose the economy can adjust on its own from the recession described in part (a) in two years. Suppose policymakers choose to use fiscal policy to stabilize the economy but the political battle over taxes and spending takes more than two years. Demonstrate these events with the model of aggregate demand and aggregate supply.

d. Describe the sequence of events shown in the graph you created in part (c) above. _____
_____
_____

e. Did the activist fiscal policy stabilize or destabilize the economy? Explain. _____
_____
_____

2. Suppose the Bank of Canada repeatedly announces that it desires price stability and that it is aiming for zero inflation. However, it consistently generates 3% inflation.

a. Will this type of behaviour on the part of the Bank of Canada reduce unemployment below the natural rate in the long run? Why? _____
_____
_____
_____

b. Once people have formed expectations of 3% inflation, what would happen in the short run if the Bank of Canada actually did achieve zero inflation? _____

_____

_____

_____

c. Would it help if Parliament passed a law requiring the Bank of Canada to target zero inflation? Why? _____

_____

_____

E. Advanced Critical Thinking

Those opposed to government budget deficits argue, among other things, that budget deficits redistribute wealth across generations by allowing the current generation to enjoy the benefits of government spending while future generations must pay for it.

1. Under which of the following cases would you argue that there is a greater intergenerational transfer of wealth? Why? _____

_____

_____

a. The government increases spending on social programs by buying apples and oranges for the poor but refuses to raise taxes, thereby, increasing the budget deficit.
b. The government increases spending on bridges, roads, and buildings but refuses to raise taxes, thereby, increasing the budget deficit.

2. Does the preceding example provide a method by which we might judge when a deficit is fair to each generation and when it is not? Explain. _____

_____

_____

_____

3. Why might this method be difficult to enforce in practice? _____

_____

_____

III. Solutions

A. True/False Questions

1. F; fiscal policy has a long lag due to the political process.
2. T
3. F; a political business cycle results when policymakers manipulate the economy to improve the incumbent's chance of re-election.

4. T
5. T
6. T
7. F; government debt redistributes wealth to the current generation from future generations.
8. F; since the mid-1970s, Canada has incurred federal budget deficits during peace and relative prosperity.
9. T
10. T

B. Multiple-Choice Questions

1. a	5. c	9. c	13. a
2. c	6. d	10. b	14. b
3. a	7. b	11. d	15. c
4. b	8. a	12. e	

C. Short-Answer Questions

1. Macroeconomic shocks need to be forecast months or years into the future because there are lags in the implementation of activist stabilization policy.

2. An independent central bank avoids the difficulties of the political business cycle and of the time inconsistency of policy.

3. Inflation imposes continuous costs on the economy such as shoeleather costs and menu costs. Reducing inflation to zero will increase unemployment only temporarily but it will eliminate the continuous costs of inflation.

4. Index the tax system and issue inflation-indexed bonds.

5. It increases future taxes and lowers future incomes by reducing the capital stock.

6. No. Redistributions of wealth across generations can be caused by many different government policies. For example, an increase in Canada Pension Plan benefits paid to the current recipients would be financed by an increase in Canada Pension Plan payroll taxes on current workers. As a result, income is transferred from younger working people to older retired people.

7. The substitution effect must outweigh the income effect. An increase in after-tax interest causes people to save more as people substitute saving for current consumption. However, the income effect of an increase in after-tax interest causes people to reduce the amount of saving necessary to reach a targeted amount of future consumption.

8. High-income people save more than low-income people so the tax relief would go disproportionately to the rich. Also, to maintain tax revenue, consumption taxes might have to be raised causing an additional burden on the poor.

D. Practice Problems

1. a.

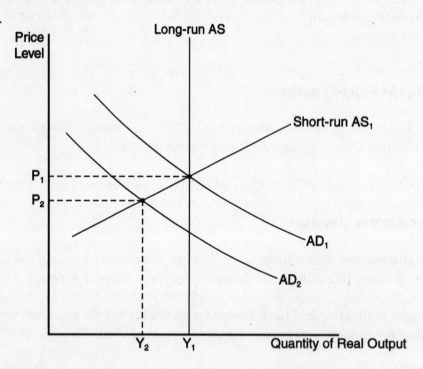

b. Increase the money supply, increase government spending, decrease taxes. Shift aggregate demand to the right.

c.

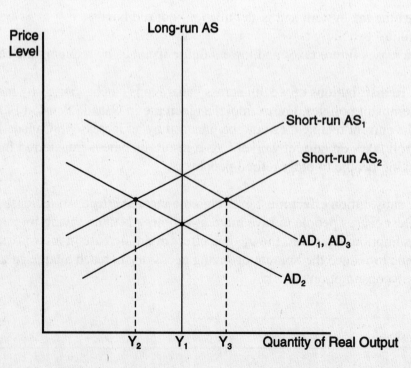

d. As short-run aggregate supply shifts to the right, the economy adjusts to the intersection of short-run AS_2 and AD_2. Then the expansionary aggregate-demand policy shifts aggregate demand to AD_3 and the economy moves to the intersection of short-run AS_2 and AD_3.

e. Destabilize, because the economy had already adjusted back to the long-run natural level so the increase in aggregate demand caused output to rise above the natural level.

2. a. No. In the long run, people will grow to expect 3% inflation and wages and prices will rise accordingly.

b. We would move down a short-run Phillips curve and inflation would fall while unemployment would rise above the natural rate.

c. Yes. The Bank of Canada's announcement of a zero inflation target would be more credible and the movement toward zero inflation would create a smaller increase in unemployment.

E. Advanced Critical Thinking

1. Case (a), because the government purchased consumption goods that cannot be enjoyed by later generations, while in case (b) the government purchased capital that is durable and can be enjoyed by later generations.

2. It is more reasonable for the government to run a deficit and force future generations to pay for current expenditures if the expenditures are for capital goods that can be used by later generations.

3. Nearly every interest group can defend their spending as if it has a positive impact on future generations — military, education, etc.